D1525759

Mindfulness and Critical Friendship

Mindfulness and Critical Friendship

A New Perspective on Professional Development for Educators

Edited by Karen Ragoonaden and Shawn Michael Bullock

LEXINGTON BOOKS
Lanham • Boulder • New York • London

Published by Lexington Books
An imprint of The Rowman & Littlefield Publishing Group, Inc.
4501 Forbes Boulevard, Suite 200, Lanham, Maryland 20706
www.rowman.com

Unit A, Whitacre Mews, 26-34 Stannary Street, London SE11 4AB

British Library Cataloguing in Publication Information Available

Library of Congress Cataloging-in-Publication Data

Names: Ragoonaden, Karen, editor. | Bullock, Shawn Michael, 1976- editor.
Title: Mindfulness and critical friendship : a new perspective on professional development for educa-
    tors / edited by Karen Ragoonaden and Shawn Michael Bullock.
Description: Lanham : Lexington Books, [2016] | Includes bibliographical references and index.
Identifiers: LCCN 2016015062 (print) | LCCN 2016017084 (ebook) | ISBN 9781498529570 (cloth :
    alk. paper) | ISBN 9781498529587 (Electronic)
Subjects: LCSH: Teachers--In-service training. | Professional learning communities. | Teachers--
    Professional relationships.
Classification: LCC LB1731 .M5545 2016 (print) | LCC LB1731 (ebook) | DDC 370.71/1--dc23 LC
    record available at https://lccn.loc.gov/2016015062

Printed in the United States of America

Table of Contents

Introduction

Mindfulness and Critical Friendship: A New Perspective on Professional Development for Educators

Karen Ragoonaden

This collection assembles an international community of scholar-practitioners from across disciplines, methodologies, and ideological perspectives reflecting on and interrogating contexts that situate mindfulness and critical friendship as constructs that support professional development for educators. Loughran (2014) states that the professional development of teacher educators must be "purposefully conceptualized, thoughtfully implemented, and meaningfully employed" (p. 11). In order to make the journey more appealing and manoeuvrable, his proposed framework illustrates how professional development for educators relates to identity, scholarship, knowledge, skill and ability. Further, he posits that an interactive, reflective exploration of self and practice can sustain teacher educators as they shape and manipulate their own professional development.

Acknowledging that John Dewey (1938) called for teachers to engage in *reflective action* and that Donald Schön (1983; 1987) depicted professional practice as a cognitive process of framing and exploring problems identified by educators for educators, this contributed volume positions that existing synergies present in mindfulness, self-study, and critical friendship are important components in not only developing the inner life and inner wisdom of educators, but also serving as organic and emergent frames upon which to situate professional development. Considering the import of Dewey's (1938) wise words and Russell's (1997) interpretation of Schön's reflection-in-action as "the reflection is in the action" (p. 15), Loughran's approach stipulating the unfolding of a practice in new ways is indicative of emergent new perspectives grounded in an agency of change.

Mindfulness has entered into contemporary consciousness largely through the work of Jon Kabat-Zinn, PhD, a molecular biologist who adapted Eastern meditative practices to clinical contexts. Arising from historical roots of the Buddhist tradition of movement in meditation, Kabat-Zinn (1990) developed and evaluated the first structured secular mindfulness-based program called Mindfulness-Based Stress Reduction (MBSR). Over the last twenty-five years, a growing body of empirical substantiation has emerged supporting the efficacy of MBSR programs into a variety of clinical fields like psychology, medicine, healthcare, and more recently, education (Baer, 2003; Ludwig and Kabat-Zinn, 2008; Shapiro and Carlson, 2009).

The initial results stemming from several mindfulness-based teacher training initiatives indicate that personal training in mindfulness skills can increase educators' sense of well-being, resiliency, and self-efficacy, as well as their ability to manage classroom behavior and establish and maintain supportive relationships with students and colleagues (Meiklejohn et al., 2012; Roeser et al., 2012; Soloway, 2011). Concomitantly, a subset of studies point to significant benefits of mindfulness practices in developing focus, attention, working memory, and academic performance (Jha et al., 2007; Mrazek et al., 2013; Tang et al., 2014). These salient findings from clinical medicine, behavioral medicine, and neuroscience have been informing the educational sciences in important ways and, by virtue of this transdisciplinary approach, have implications for educational practice and policy (Mackenzie, 2015). Consequently, Mindfulness Training (MT) resources have been applied to educational contexts in order to maximize the mental, emotional, physical, and psychological benefits provided by this holistic mind-body approach to well-being.

Beck, Freese, and Kosnik (2004) describe self-study as an inquiry-oriented approach that is personal, reflective, collaborative, and constructivist. By identifying a personalized focus of inquiry, a strong sense of purpose motivated by a deep need to understand and to reflect on practice emerges. The constructive element of self-study pertains to the ongoing inquiry leading to new paradigms of practice, as well as the acknowledgment of personal experience on practice. In particular, self-study's aim to "provoke, challenge, and illuminate rather than conform and settle" (Bullough and Pinnegar, 2001, p. 20) points to the critically informed discourses that can arise. At present, self-study is recognized as an emergent methodology in teacher educators' personal and professional growth characterized through its self-initiation and focus on improvement (LaBoskey, 2007; Macintyre and Buck, 2007). Since self-study is founded upon the belief that teaching is fundamentally an autobiographical act, self-knowledge is important for transforming pedagogy and practice. This type of critical reflection provides opportunities for modelling reflection and seeking alternate rhetoric to improve practice (Samaras et al., 2007). Through this approach, educators can examine self-knowing and professional identity formation in their practice and its impact on student learning. Self-study's holistic approach to personal and professional explorations is a natural pathway towards integrating and interconnecting principles of concepts of mindfulness and well-being into educational practice.

In keeping with the focus on developing criticality in a progressive scaffolding of ideas, concepts, and epistemologies, critical friendship viewed through a mindfulness lens builds upon previous experience through reflection and revision facilitating and promoting transformative pedagogy and practice. By reflecting on significant professional events and analyzing these circumstances, teacher educators can focus on developing successful strategies which explore pathways between knowledge and praxis particularly in non-traditional educational contexts. Mindfulness and critical friendship can prove to be a rite of passage in professional development allowing educators to connect critically and creatively with like-minded colleagues. Critical friendships, therefore, must be nurtured in a mindful climate of trust, compassion, and empathy, encouraging analysis, integrity, and culminating in an advocacy for success, necessary conditions for the emergence of a sustained professional development.

In the following chapters, the authors examine contexts in which mindfulness and critical friendship provide a framework for educators to interrogate and question the practice and praxis of professional development. Supported by a robust set of evidence-based research, the content of this volume considers ways in which to develop habits of mind and courses of action that support educators as they cultivate competencies for thriving and coping with the modern demands of their lived and professional lives. Acquiescing to the wisdom of inner life, appraising the parallels between mindfulness and critical friendship, reflecting on the impact of relational pedagogy and philosophy and, finally, questioning the ubiquitous presence of Mindfulness/McMindfulness in educational spheres, this collection concludes with a considered response promoting the cultivation of kindness as an act of intentional professional development.

In *Inner Wisdom: A Foundation for Being a Teacher*, Falkenberg theorizes that the inner life of, and the inner work for teachers draw on existing practices of "mind work" (e.g., mindfulness practices). He develops the notion of inner wisdom as a foundation for professional development of educators. This chapter takes its starting point in the assumptions that at the core of teaching is the direct engagement of teacher and student(s). The anchor upon which such engagement happens is the functioning of the teacher's "inner life" (feelings, thoughts, intentions, etc.) at the very moment of engagement. Consequently, a teacher's capacity to do "inner work" (working on and with what we attend to and notice of our inner life) becomes of central importance to the unfolding of practice.

Critical Friends: The Practiced Wisdom of Professional Development introduces and discusses the seminal concepts of identity, culture, and knowledge construction in higher education. Framed as a collaborative online self-study, Ragoonaden and Bullock utilize the metaphors of border-crossings to explicate and to position critical friendship as professional development for teacher educators. Taking their cue from Dunne (1993), practical wisdom provided a lens upon to examine practice and praxis. While recognizing the importance of *techne* in this endeavour, they also searched for a substantive process which would awaken and entice their conceptions of *phronesis* (practical and moral knowledge). By deconstructing epistemological abstractions, they progressed towards new knowledge and clarified understandings and tensions not only in their own practices but in practices outside their own.

Collaborative self-study coupled with critical friendship proved to be a rite of passage in their professional development allowing them to connect critically and creatively. The diverse dimensions of critical friendship in collaborative self-study demonstrate that this type of supported inquiry is malleable and flexible enough to mold itself into to multiple contexts of professional development.

In *Critical Friendship as Mindful and Relational Professional Development,* Schnellert and Richardson utilize a personalized stance to explore practice. Reflecting on their ten-year personal and professional relationship, the authors explore the intersections of their PhD studies, narrative and arts-based inquiries, experiences co-teaching, and co-researching. Reunited in the same Faculty of Education, they experienced the launch of a significant mindfulness initiative. As scholar-practitioners who take up mindfulness in their lives, scholarship, and pedagogies, they struggled to comprehend a mindfulness discourse that seemed to further a neo-liberal agenda. Emanating from long-term mindfulness practices and critically-reflective scholarship, they engaged in intellectual and experiential understandings of mindful pedagogy and research as constituted through responsive, participatory, and social justice-oriented praxis. This chapter explores how they negotiated their work within this university context while seeking to maintain social justice aims through situated and reflexive approaches to inquiry.

Critical Friends, Critical Insights: Developing a Dialogic Understanding of Practice-Based Teacher Education emphasizes the meaningful connections between theory and practice. As critical friends, Rut Gísladóttir, Johnson Lachuk, and DeGraff, describe individual challenges and successes in engaging with practice-based methods. Sustained by their enduring relationships in Iceland and the United States respectively, this collaborative self-study provided the space to create a professional international context where discussions, challenges, and shared experiences could inform practice. To generate data, each author composed, shared, and discussed four narratives about their lived stories as literacy teacher educators enacting practice-based methods. Using a Readers Theater format, they identified key elements from their recorded and transcribed narratives, then purposefully reconstructed these data to find common themes.

Findings illuminate how the dialogic process of sharing and interpreting stories facilitated an ongoing reflection of practices and provided sustainable professional development initiatives for colleagues working in international contexts limited by time and space.

Critical Friendship, Mindfulness, and the Philosophy for Children Hawai'i Approach to Teaching and Learning investigates how the philosophy for children Hawai'i approach to teaching and learning promotes critical friendship and mindfulness in five teacher educators from the USA, Taiwan, Canada, and China. United by their collective interests in p4cHI, Strong Makaiau, Wang, Ragoonaden, Leng, and DeWoody use self-study methodologies to create an *intellectually safe* online journaling community to engage in a critical examination of actions and contexts as a pathway towards professional activity. In this chapter, methods of constant comparison are used to analyze how the core features of p4cHI (e.g., not being in a rush, respect, sensitivity to context, wonderment, dialogue, presence, and self-reflection) enabled the researchers to co-construct a community of critical friendship and to engage collectively in a mindful process that deepened the understanding of self, other, and professional practice.

Critical Friendship and Meta-Critical Friendship: Re-Interrogating Assumptions characterizes how a unique three-way critical friendship (Déirdre and Mary from Ireland and Tim from Canada) supported the development, implementation and research of a pedagogical innovation in physical education teacher education (PETE). Across a two-year period Tim and Déirdre experimented with the pedagogical innovation with undergraduate classes in Canada and Ireland. They acted as critical friends to each other: sharing weekly reflective journal entries and recorded Skype conversations. After identifying "turning points" shared initially with each other, they then shared these episodes with their third critical friend, Mary. Mary, an experienced PETE practitioner and researcher offered an additional layer of analytical engagement—a type of "meta-critical friend" engaged in a *Third Space* (Bhabha, 1994). Her role was to support and critique the pedagogical innovation and focus the line of inquiry by asking "so what?" questions during three-way Skype dialogues. The potential of incorporating the novel concept of a "meta-critical friend" to support innovative pedagogical development and practices is explored in this chapter.

Cultivating a Mindfulness for McMindfulness acknowledges that mainstream Mindfulness in education has reached epic proportions in contemporary consciousness. Embraced and practiced in schools throughout North America, its unfolding presence is making its way into pre-service, in-service teacher and graduate education programs. The author, Gilham, posits that it is paramount for participants to be critically aware and to analyze the diverse interpretations and instances of Mindfulness in Education (MIE). Since, most predominant discussions extol the benefits and increasing evidence in support of MIE, a much needed level of scholarly inquiry can add an element of validity to the ongoing positive discourses. For example, a number of researchers are interrogating the various ways in which secular interpretations of Mindfulness are disseminated in the West. Since some Western conceptions of Mindfulness are untethered from historical Eastern systems, a number of scholars have introduced the term *McMindfulness* into academic parlance. Arguments propound that MIE can be advanced unknowingly in instrumental and rationalized ways that reinforce Western notions of individuality, efficiency, and docility, and the ever increasing therapeutic milieu of schools. This is in direct contradiction to the seminal concepts of kindness, empathy, and forgiveness prevalent in Mindfulness epistemology.

In *Kindness: A Mindful Act of Well-Being,* Binfet explores the relationship between social and emotional well-being, mindfulness and professional development. He reiterates the importance of professional development as a holistic approach focusing on the entire individual, progressing away from academic abilities or workplace technical proficiencies. In order to create learning environments and communities that foster wellbeing among all educational stakeholders, the act of incorporating initiatives grounded in mindfulness and the encouragement of *Intentional Acts of Kindness* (IAK) hold the potential to build social and emotional competencies that carry from the classroom to the boardroom. The immediate effects are classroom and school communities where introspection, consideration of others, and intentional kindness flourish. The long-term effects support employees whose soft and hard skills, whose technical proficiencies, and social and emotional competencies support workplace productivity, retention, and individual and collective well-being.

As indicated, the chapters presented in this volume introduce the concept of mindfulness coupled with critical friendship as an evidence-based initiative supporting a comprehensive approach to professional development. The content of this collection examines ways in which to develop habits of mind that support educators as they cultivate the abilities, competencies and skills that nurture their inner and outer lives. The overarching purpose is to examine the inherent complexities, challenges, and potential rewards of introducing emergent and organic elements of critical friendship married to secular conceptions of Mindfulness as a multifaceted approach to improving pedagogical practice for educators.

REFERENCES

Baer, Ruth A. (2003). Mindfulness Training as a Clinical Intervention: A Conceptual and Empirical Review. *Clinical Psychology: Science and Practice* 10, no. 2: 125–43.
Beck, C., Freese, A., and Kosnik, C. (2004). The preservice practicum: Learning through self-study in a professional setting. In J. J. Loughran, M. L. Hamilton, V. K.

LaBoskey, and T. Russell (Eds.), *International handbook of self-study of teaching and teacher education practices* (pp. 1259–93). Dordrecht: Kluwer.

Bhabha, H. (1994) *The Location of Culture.* New York: Routledge.

Bullough, R. V. J., and Pinnegar, S. (2001). Guidelines for quality in autobiographical forms of self-study research. *Educational Researcher* 30, no. 3: 13–21

Dewey, J. (1938). *Experience and education.* New York: Collier Books.

Dunne, J. (1993). *Back to the rough ground: Practical judgment and the lure of technique.* Notre Dame: University of Notre Dame Press.

Jha, Amishi P., Jason Krompinger, and Michael J. Baime. (2007). Mindfulness Training Modifies Subsystems of Attention. *Cognitive, Affective, & Behavioral Neuroscience* 7, no. 2: 109–19.

Kabat-Zinn, J. (1990). *Full catastrophe of living.* New York: Bantam Books.

LaBoskey, V. K. (2007). The methodology of self-study and its theoretical underpinnings. In J. J. Loughran, M. L. Hamilton, V. K. LaBoskey, and T. Russell (Eds.), *International handbook of self-study of teaching and teacher education practices* (pp. 817–69). Dordrecht: Kluwer.

Loughran, J. (2014). Professionally Developing as a Teacher Educator. *Journal of Teacher Education* 65, no. 4: 271–83.

Ludwig, David S., and Jon Kabat-Zinn. Mindfulness in Medicine. (2008). *Journal of the American Medical Association* 300, no. 11, 1350–52.

Macintyre, L., and Buck, L. (2007). Professional development risks and opportunities embodied within self-study. *Studying Teacher Education* 3, no. 2: 189–205.

MacKenzie, E. (2015). Mindfulness Training: A transdiciplinary approach to assessing efficacy in education. In Ragoonaden, K. (2015). *Mindful teaching and learning: Developing a pedagogy of well-being.* Lanham, MD: Lexington Books.

Meiklejohn, John, Catherine Phillips, M. Lee Freedman, Mary Lee Griffin, Gina Biegel, Andy Roach, Jenny Frank et al. (2012). Integrating Mindfulness Training into K–12 Education: Fostering the Resilience of Teachers and Students. *Mindfulness* 3, no. 4: 291–307.

Mrazek, Michael D., Michael S. Franklin, Dawa Tarchin Phillips, Benjamin Baird, and Jonathan W. Schooler. (2013). Mindfulness Training Improves Working Memory Capacity and GRE Performance while Reducing Mind Wandering. *Psychological Science*: 0956797612459659.

Roeser, R. W., Skinner, E., Beers, J. and Jennings, P. A. (2012). Mindfulness Training and Teachers' Professional Development: An Emerging Area of Research and Practice. *Child Development Perspectives* 6: 167–73. DOI: 10.1111/j.1750-8606.2012.00238.x

Roeser, Robert W., Kimberly A. Schonert-Reichl, Amishi Jha, Margaret Cullen, Linda Wallace, Rona Wilensky, Eva Oberle, Kimberly Thomson, Cynthia Taylor, and Jessica Harrison. (2013). Mindfulness Training and Reductions in Teacher Stress and Burnout: Results from Two Randomized, Waitlist-Control Field Trials. *Journal of Educational Psychology* 105, no. 3: 787.

Russell, T. (1997). Teaching teachers. How I teach IS the message. In J. Loughran and T. Russell (Eds.), *Teaching about teaching: Purpose, passion and pedagogy in teacher education* (pp. 32–47). London: Falmer Press.

Samaras, A., Hicks, M., and Garvey Berger, J. (2004). Self-study through personal history. In J. J. Loughran, M. L. Hamilton, V. K. LaBoskey, and T. Russell (Eds.), *International handbook of self-study of teaching and teacher education practices* (pp. 905–42). Dordrecht: Kluwer.

Schön, D. (1983). *The reflective practitioner: How professionals think in action.* San Francisco: Jossey-Bass.

Schön, D. (1987). *Educating the reflective practitioner.* San Francisco: Jossey-Bass.

Shapiro, S. L., and Carlson, L. E. (2009). *The art and science of mindfulness: Integrating mindfulness into psychology and the helping professions.* Washington, DC: American Psychological Association.

Soloway, G. B. (2011). Preparing teachers for the present: Exploring the praxis of mindfulness training in teacher education. Unpublished doctoral dissertation, University of Toronto, Ontario.

Tang, Y. Y., R. Tang, C. Jiang, and M. I. Posner. (2014). Short-Term Meditation Intervention Improves Self-Regulation and Academic Performance. *Journal of Child Adolescent Behavior* 2, no. 154: 2.

ONE

Inner Wisdom

A Foundation for Being a Teacher

Thomas Falkenberg

In keeping with the theme of mindfulness and self-study through critical friendship as important components of professional development, this chapter is concerned with the functioning of our mind and our mind's role in who we are and how we respond, act, and behave as teachers as we encounter our students.[1] To illustrate this concern, let me start with a vignette.

Picture a teacher educator teaching a class of teacher candidates in a classroom. She has just assigned a task to them to undertake in groups of four. After having given the instructions to the students, the teacher educator looks around the room, taking in the image of students getting in groups and starting to work on the task. No particular thought occupies the teacher educator's mind at that moment, when she notices a particular student getting ready to sit down. Suddenly an episode from last class comes to her mind, when she observed that student clandestinely using her cellphone during an activity. The teacher educator's heart starts beating faster and a feeling of uneasiness arises in her; she feels a slight contraction in her stomach area. The thought comes to her mind that this student does not seem to take the course seriously, and that she should monitor this student today. Suddenly her attention shifts to an approaching student, who is starting to ask her something. The teacher educator turns to her, and thoughts related to the question start dominating her mind, while the feeling of uneasiness still persists. When the student has left, suddenly the lesson plan and the timing come to the teacher educator's mind, and she turns to the clock on the wall and notices that she is about ten minutes behind her planned schedule.

The vignette speaks of *images* and *thoughts* that suddenly *come to mind*, and of *feelings* that suddenly arise, about a *shift of attention* and of *noticing*, and how attention is drawn away toward a new object of attention.

The vignette illustrates what I—and others—call "the inner life" (see, for instance, Cohen, 2009/2015; Johnson, 1986). This chapter is about teachers' inner lives and the role those inner lives can and do play in teaching, and how that might impact our understanding of what it means to be a teacher. There are three theses that this chapter will develop: 1. A teacher's inner life plays a central role in how she engages with her students. 2. Teachers can and should learn to attend to their inner life in order to address the ethical imperative of teaching. 3. With a greater concern for teachers' inner lives a distinction between "to teach" (doing) and "being a teacher" (being) becomes more prominent for teaching. Each thesis will be developed in one of the subsequent three sections.

INNER LIFE

The vignette from the introduction illustrates "inner life" at work. In a first approximation I like to suggest that "inner life" is characterized by what is going on in our mind: sensations, feelings, images, thoughts, and intentions. I start with five observations of our inner life.

Five Observations

The first observation is that *our inner life is "the very stuff of our lives"* (Varela, 1999, p. 9).

> We *always* operate in some kind of immediacy of a given situation. Our lived world is so ready-at-hand that we have no deliberateness about what it is and how we inhabit it. When we sit at the table to eat with a relative or friend, the entire complex know-how of how to handle our utensils, how to sit, how to convers, is present without deliberation. (Varela, 1999, p. 9)

Such immediacy of a given situation and the availability and use of know-how for acting and responding in such situations in the moment permeates the living of our lives—as teachers or humans more generally. While *acting* in response to a given situation can be non-immediate, delayed or even avoided, our *inner life* is always operating in the immediacy of a given situation—and situations are given to us as part of our inner life, namely as thoughts, images, feelings, and so on. Varela (1999) suggests that the know-how that is available to us in a situation of a certain type creates a "microidentity" for us (p. 10), something that characterizes who we are in such types of situations. This suggests a core role of our inner life in who we are as a person and a teacher.

The second observation is that *we can be—and often are—unaware of our inner life in given situations*. While our responding in situations is framed by what we perceive of the situation, such perceptions of outer or inner-sourced experiences can and often are at the subconscious level. As Lakoff and Johnson (1999) suggest, "it is the rule of thumb among cognitive scientists that unconscious thought is 95 percent of all thought" (p. 13). There are numerous examples, demonstrating how often subconscious know-how is enacted as we respond to the immediacy of a given situation.[2]

I am not saying here that we do not know what we are doing. We do, but in a specific sense. Our know-how allows us to respond in the immediacy of a given situation. We are acting-in-the-situation, our focus and attention is oriented toward the acting in the situation. As has been pointed out in the Buddhist psychology of the mind, however, there is a crucial difference between thinking a thought and being aware of thinking the thought; similarly, there is a difference between feeling an emotion and being aware of the feeling (Gunaratana, 2002, pp. 70, 140). For instance, let us assume that I notice a teacher candidate with bright yellow hair in the hallway. I might think "This man seeks attention from others." In this situation I am *thinking the thought* that this man seeks attention from others. However, I can also be aware of that very thought, in which case I might notice with interest how my structure of prejudices links a particular hair color to an assumed psychological need. Thinking the thought is my inner life at work. Being aware of that thought is *conscious awareness* of my inner life. This marks a crucial distinction between "living our inner life" through enacting our know-how in the immediacy of a situation and our conscious awareness of our inner life. This chapter is focused on the latter.

It is often what we call "routines" that escape our conscious awareness. These routines help us cope with the immediacy of the situations that make up our lives, but they can also be problematic—a point that I will discuss later.

The third observation is that *we can be aware of our inner life in given situations*. This seems particularly the case where we experience extreme shifts to what we consider "normal" in a given situation. For instance, when we feel bodily pain, when thoughts and intentions arise that extremely violate what we consider to be our ethical principles, or when our body responds to sad news we just received by increasing our heart rate and cramping our abdominal muscles.

The fourth observation is that *we can learn to become more aware of our inner life as it unfolds in a given moment*. For instance, contemplative practices in different so-called wisdom traditions are in part about becoming more aware of one's inner life. For instance, relative recent research in the cognitive and brain sciences in the West on the impact of mindfulness practices on the brain structure and mind capacities strongly suggests that those practices indeed can help us become more aware of our inner life in given situations (see, for instance, Austin, 2009; Shapiro and Carlson, 2009; Smalley and Winston, 2010). I want to call—following other scholars—the working on our awareness of our inner life "inner work" (see, for instance, Cohen, 2009/2015; Johnson, 1986).

The fifth observation is that *our inner life has an ethical aspect*. I would even go so far to claim that our inner life is at the core of who we are as ethical beings. If our inner life is partially our response to our perception of the outer world and is also the basis upon which we respond to and act in that world—as I suggested above—then our inner life has clearly an ethical aspect. It is through our responding to our thinking, feeling, and intentions that we engage with the world, including our fellow humans. In other words, it is our inner life that shapes *how* we engage with the world and, thus, it shapes who we are as ethical beings.

Automatic Routines and the Ethical Imperative of Teaching

Considering the importance of our inner life for who we are as a teacher and person more generally, the level of awareness of our inner life, what aspects of our inner life we are attending to, what we notice of our inner life and the routines through which we enact our know-how to cope with the demands of a given situation all seem of great importance to our capacity to work with and on our inner life.[3] The following vignette—adapted from Falkenberg (2012, p. 5)—is to help illustrate their importance.

> It is shortly before the end of class, and the teacher is talking to the students, explaining something. The teacher looks at the clock on the wall and suddenly feels rushed for time. She speeds up her talking, and while she talks, a student raises his hand and says something at the same time. The teacher shushes the student; suddenly the teacher feels blood rushing into her face and a slight cramp-like feeling in her chest area. While she continues talking, the teacher notices her blushing, and then feels slight cramping in the stomach area. She feels distracted from her talking to the students; she finishes off her explanation and gives some instructions for work to the students for the last three minutes of class. As the teacher turns around and goes to sitting down at her desk, thoughts about the 'incident' become more prominent and then take over her mind as she sits down.

Let me first comment on this vignette in terms of the role of awareness, attention, and noticing and of automatic routines in teaching. The teacher *attends to* the clock on the wall, *notices* the time and speeds up her talking; this is an example of *awareness that enables action*. She also feels rushed, which is an example of *awareness* triggering physiological responses. The shushing of the student is *action enabled by the teacher's conscious awareness* of the student's interruption of her talking. While she is talking, part of her *attention is drawn* to her physiological state: she *notices* her blushing. This *awareness* triggers thoughts about the "incident," which is an example of *awareness enabling action*, in this case the arising of thoughts. In terms of routines, the teacher's attending to the clock on the wall might be automatic behavior, routine behavior by an experienced teacher who might have a "sense" for timing. Second, the teacher's speeding up in response to noticing the time might be an automatic response by the teacher. Furthermore, the shushing seems to clearly have come as an automatic response. As well, the emotional, physiological response to the shushing—the blushing and the feelings in the chest and stomach areas—seem automatic responses to what the teacher has become consciously aware of in these moments.

Such routines have tremendous advantages for our coping with all the immediacies that we face in teaching and life more generally. Routine expertise in teaching (see, for instance, Berliner, 2001) is seen by teacher education scholars as being of great importance for quality teaching (see, for instance, Darling-Hammond and Bransford, 2005). The know-how that allows us to adequately cope in the immediacy of a situation is grounded in such routines. But routines have *dis*advantages, exactly for the reason they provide us often with an advantage: they are un-controlled. As teachers—and as human beings more generally—what we want is (a) having available to us the right routines at the right time in the right situation and (b) the ability to change problematic routines. This is one of the concerns for inner work for teachers and a central characteristic of inner wisdom as I will explicate below.

Let me now comment on the vignette in terms of the ethical imperative of teaching. This imperative is grounded in the idea that teaching is an ethical endeavor because "teaching . . . is, quite centrally, human action undertaken in regard to other human beings" (Fenstermacher, 1990, p. 133). The inner life of the teacher in the vignette takes a particular turn after the automatic shushing of the student: She notices physiological responses right after, and thoughts about the shushing incident first become more prominent and then take over her thinking at the end of the vignette. These developments of the teacher's inner life might be interpreted as a disturbance of the flow in which "thinking, feeling and wanting all go together and lead to effective behaviour" (Korthagen, 2013, p. 35). One way in which this disturbance of flow can be interpreted is that the teacher's automatic shushing response was in conflict with her deep seated values, that is, her understanding of the ethical imperative of teaching. Our inner life is characterized by patterns of thinking, feeling, and by drives, which manifest in how we behave and act in such personal encounters and pedagogical moments with our students. Understanding our inner life is, thus, important for our understanding of the ethical imperative as teachers. Parker Palmer (1998) suggests that we teach who we are. If that is indeed the case, we better be concerned with who we are as teachers and, thus, with our inner life. This concern for our inner life as teachers leads to the practical concern for our capacity for "inner work," which I will turn to now.

INNER WORK

Conceptualizing Inner Work

Quite a while back I was introduced to the idea of inner work in the sense relevant here by my colleague and friend Avraham Cohen (2009/2015):

> The term *inner work* refers to reflective practices conducted under the gaze of consciousness, which depends on a developed capacity to self-observe, to witness experience. . . . Inner work is a way of working on and with perceptions, sensations, memories, and cognitions, all of which constitute a person's experience. (p. 29)

Simplified, we can say that inner work is the practice of working with one's inner life.

For the context of teaching, the purpose of inner work is to develop our capacity to be aware of, attend to, and notice our inner life as it unfolds as we teach in order to address the ethical imperative of teaching. What can such inner work for teachers look like?[4]

Attending to Inner Experiences

In order to work with our inner life as teachers we need to develop our capacity to attend to our inner life, that is, to attend to the objects that make up our mind: our sensations, feelings, images, thoughts, and intentions—let me call them for short "inner experiences." There are a number of types of inner work approaches in teacher education. Some approaches within the self-study of teacher education practices movement and the practical wisdom approaches to teacher education are examples. They provide practices that are of great value *for the reflection component* of the inner work for teachers. For instance, there is the *intelligent report of experience* practice proposed as a way to develop teacher candidates' capacity for discernment in the practical wisdom approach by Anne Phelan (2005), and there is the *coaching based on core reflection* practice proposed by Korthagen and his collaborators in their Core Reflection Approach to teacher education (Hoekstra and Korthagen, 2013). What these approaches to inner work have in common is that teachers attend to their inner experiences through reflection in the sense of Schön's (1983) reflection-on-action. While reflection is an important component of inner work, when re-flecting we re-create, re-member, or re-imagine those inner experiences *after* the original inner experiences have happened and *outside* of the immediate situational contexts in which those experiences arose. Rather I am interested here in that aspect of inner work that involves our capacity to attend to our inner experiences *while* we are teaching and *as* we have those experiences *within* the specific situational context. Why is such a capacity important to teaching? Let me provide two reasons.

First, the use of reflection on past experiences always involves a form of re-creating of these original inner experiences, which means, in reflection activities we are always creating new inner experiences that we think and hope are similar enough to the original inner experiences we try to re-create, to re-member. I suggest now that if we as teachers have developed our capacity to attend to our inner experiences *as* we have those experiences, we will be able to more accurately re-create those experiences when we reflect on them. While I am not aware of any studies that inquired into this particular link, my own experience with inner work and my attending to my inner experiences as I have them strongly support the link.

The second reason for developing our capacity to attend to our inner experiences as we have them is directly linked to the role of this capacity for a particular approach to inner work for teachers. Let me first outline this particular approach and then identify the role that this capacity plays in the approach. In Falkenberg (2012) I have outlined an approach I called "teaching as contemplative professional practice." This practice is conceptualized as professional practice that involves on-going inquiry into our inner lives as teachers. The big idea behind this approach to inner work in and for teaching is as follows. As teachers our acting-in-the-moment of teacher-students encounters is framed by the state of our inner life at that very moment. We cannot expect of us that our inner life, our acting, and our automatic routines and know-hows are always completely in line with our ethical commitment to teaching in general and to our students in particular. Through our understanding of our inner life or through reflection on our teaching action, including our routines, we might identify aspects of our inner life that we need or should work on to bring it in line with our ethical commitment to teaching. We, thus, engage in practices that help us develop our understanding and working with and on our inner life in a desired way. This is the inner work involved in teaching as contemplative professional practice.

Our capacity to attend to our inner experiences at the time of their occurrence plays an important role in this approach to inner work. Let me illustrate the role by drawing on the vignette from above of the teacher who shushes one of her students. The teacher was able to attend to an inner experience as it occurred, namely her physiological response to her shushing: the blushing and the cramping in her stomach and chest area. In the reflection part of her inner work, she might decide that shushing her student in this moment was not the right thing to do; she thinks that she should not have felt to be under time pressure and as a consequence dismiss her student in the way she did. She decides to work on the way she experiences time and not to try to feel pressured by time so that she can properly address her students' needs. In order to work on the way she experiences time, she would do the following: First, she would imagine alternative ways of feeling and acting. Then she would try to notice specific types of inner experiences, namely feelings of time pressure, as they start to arise. She needs to notice these before they arise, so she might have a chance to respond differently to her students in these moments. Obviously, for this purpose, her ability to attend to her inner experiences as they arise is crucial. Without this ability it will be almost impossible to notice the inner experience of feeling time pressure in time to have alternative ways of responding available to her. How can we develop our capacity to attend to our inner experiences?

Mindfulness Meditation

Over 2,000 years ago, Buddhist psychology has developed an understanding of our mind and, based on this understanding, has developed practices that indeed can help people develop such capacity: mindfulness meditation practices (see, for instance, Gunaratana, 2002; Shapiro and Walsh, 1984; Smalley and Winston, 2010). "Being mindful" in this tradition means to be *pre-conceptually and non-judgmentally aware of one's present inner experiences* (see, for instance Kabat-Zinn, 2005, pp. 108–9). The practices developed in Buddhist psychology to enhance one's ability to be mindful have demonstrable impact on that ability (see, for instance, Siegel, 2007). To be mindful while teaching will give us the opportunity to notice our inner life without having to immediately respond to the noticing of physiological changes, particular thoughts and feelings that arise in particular moments of our teaching. Being mindful while teaching provides us with the opportunity to observe our inner life while we are in the flow of teaching.

Buddhist psychology has developed two types of meditation practice that seem of particular value to developing our capacity to attend to our inner experiences: receptive meditation and concentrative meditation (see Austin, 2009, p. 4). Receptive meditation involves practices in which practitioners attend to the thoughts, images, intentions, or sensations as those arise in one's mind. The purpose of receptive meditation practices is pure observation, ideally involving no conceptualizing of the experience and no judgment of the experience. The concentration meditation involves practices in which the practitioner attends to one particular object of attention and tries to stay attentively with that object for a given period of time. Often the focus of attention is a particular aspect of one's breathing, for instance, the place in the nostril where the burst of air one breathes in and then out is passing by.

The ongoing practice of inquiring into our inner experiences together with the insights resulting from such practice for the purpose of addressing the ethical imperative of our living characterizes what I would call *inner wisdom*.[5] In the next section I argue that such inner wisdom should be considered a foundational aspect of what it means *to be* a teacher.

BEING A TEACHER

What does it mean to be a teacher? In an opinion piece written in 1992, Ken Osborn (as quoted in Young, Levin, and Wallin, 2007, pp. 279–80) has argued that teachers and their associations should see themselves *primarily* as public employees and unions, respectively, rather than as professionals and their professional associations, respectively. He argues that because school education is values-based and purpose-driven, school education—its purpose and method—is primarily the responsibility of the community and its elected representatives; teachers are employees of the public serving those values, purposes, and methods. Teachers as employees are hired because of the craftspersonship that they have developed and that they are paid to employ to serve those values, purposes, and methods.

In contrast to this understanding of what it means to be a teacher there is a much earlier notion of "teacher," a notion that might have had its historical pinnacle at what the German philosopher Karl Jaspers (1953) has called "the axial age," which was the age in which many religious philosophers like Buddha, Jesus, Mohammed, and others where teaching. Here, being a teacher meant being a "master" to one's "disciples." Under the header "the Zen master," Lasalle (1968/1974) wrote:

> We come now to the guidance imparted by the Zen master which is of vital significance for Zen. The relationship between the master and the disciple has always been closer in the Orient than in the Occident. This is especially evident in the practice of Zen. For the great experience, *satori*, is not imparted by means of the written word, but through *ishin-denshin*: from mind to mind. . . .
>
> The guidance or transmission mediated by the Zen master is important not only for the continuation of the tradition in the very great figures of Zen Buddhism, but in every individual case where a disciple studies under a master as well. And the same principle applies here: *ishin-denshin*, direct transmission by the person, and not by the written word. This method ensures that the essence of the experience is not falsified. . . . Zen requires personal guidance from the very beginning, for the disciple attempts to penetrate to the unconscious from the outset. (pp. 20–21)

For this reason, it was not uncommon practice that disciples would move in with their teacher, an approach to teaching and learning that is still practiced for the same reasons, because "all learning of non-trivial subjects is at the foundation tacit, embodied, and involves the whole personality" (Bai, 2006, p. 17). In this tradition, the teacher teaches by *being* the person she is and students learn the "non-trivial subjects" by being around and with the teacher. For Osborn the teacher is *doing* her job, employing the quality of her craftspersonship in a particular field of study.

The current understanding of what it means to be a teacher in Canada does not go quite as far as Osborn suggests. What speaks to that is the widespread understanding of teaching as a profession—especially in the profession itself—and the existence of codes of ethics for teachers and professional suitability policies for teacher candidates in at least some Canadian faculties of education. On the other hand, this widespread understanding of the teacher as a professional does not go as far as the understanding of what it means to be a teacher reported on by Lasalle and Bai.

The role of teachers' inner lives—and, thus, the role of teachers' inner work—is quite different in the two extreme cases to the degree that this role characterizes a central distinction between a "doing" approach to teaching and a "being" approach to teaching. If we accept that we "teach, who we are" (Palmer, 1998) and—as I would add—"who we are is *what* we teach," then this suggests a much greater role for teachers' "inner wisdom" for our understanding of teaching than a doing approach to teaching seems to allow for. It is in the being approach to teaching where the ethical imperative of teaching is front and center for teaching. Here "inner wisdom" is of *foundational* importance, since it is our inner life—as argued above—that characterizes us as ethical beings.

NOTES

1. Acknowledgment: This chapter is based on my keynote address at the Annual Conference of the Canadian Association for Teacher Education (CATE) at the University of Ottawa on 2nd June 2015. I thank the Executive Committee of CATE for that opportunity.

2. See, for instance, the examples on "mindless eating" in Wansink (2006).

3. For a more technical discussion of awareness, attention and noticing in the context of inner life, see Falkenberg (2012).

4. For a more psychotherapeutic approach to inner work for educators, see Cohen (2009/2015).

5. This phrase seems quite fitting considering the way "wisdom" has been used in the context of teaching and teacher education (see, for instance, Korthagen, 2001; Shulman, 2004; Phelan, 2005).

REFERENCES

Austin, J. H. (2009). *Selfless insight: Zen and the meditative transformation of consciousness.* Cambridge, MA: MIT Press.

Bai, H. (2006). Philosophy of education: Towards human agency. *Paideusis: Journal of the Canadian Philosophy of Education Society* 15, no. 1: 7–19.

Berliner, D. C. (2001). Learning about and learning from expert teachers. *International Journal of Educational Research* 35: 463–82.

Cohen, A. (2015). *Becoming fully human within educational environments: Inner life, relationship, and learning.* Burnaby, BC: The Write Room Press. (First published 2009)

Darling-Hammond, L., and Bransford, J. (Eds.). (2005). *Preparing teachers for a changing world: What teachers should learn and be able to do.* San Francisco: Jossey-Bass.

Falkenberg, T. (2012). Teaching as contemplative professional practice. *Paideusis: The Journal of the Canadian Philosophy of Education Society* 20, no. 2: 25–35.

Fenstermacher, G. D. (1990). Some moral considerations on teaching as a profession. In J. I. Goodlad, R. Soder and K. A. Sirotnik (Eds.), *The moral dimensions of teaching* (pp. 130–51). San Francisco: Jossey-Bass.

Gunaratana, B. H. (2002). *Mindfulness in plain English* (Updated and exp. ed.). Boston: Wisdom Publications.

Hoekstra, A., and Korthagen, F. A. J. (2013). Coaching based on core reflection makes a difference. In F. A. J. Korthagen, Y. M. Kim, and W. L. Greene (Eds.), *Teaching and learning from within: A core reflection approach to quality and inspiration in education* (pp. 93–107). New York: Routledge.

Jaspers, K. (1953). *Origin and goal of history.* London: Routledge and K. Paul.

Johnson, R. A. (1986). *Inner work: Using dreams and active imagination for personal growth.* New York: HarperCollins.

Kabat-Zinn, J. (2005). *Coming to our senses: Healing ourselves and the world through mindfulness.* New York: Hyperion.

Korthagen, F. A. J. (with Kessels, J., Koster, B., Lagerwerf, B, & Wubbels, T.) (2001). *Linking practice and theory: The pedagogy of realistic teacher education.* Mahwah, NJ: Lawrence Erlbaum.

Korthagen, F. A. J. (2013). The core reflection approach. In F. A. J. Korthagen, Y. M. Kim, and W. L. Greene (Eds.), *Teaching and learning from within: A core reflection approach to quality and inspiration in education* (pp. 24–41). New York: Routledge.

Lakoff, G., and Johnson, M. (1999). *Philosophy in the flesh: The embodied mind and its challenge to western thought.* New York: Basic Books.

Lasalle, H. M. E. (1974). *Zen meditation for Christians* (J. C. Maraldo, Trans.). La Salle, IL: Open Court. (Originally published 1968)

Palmer, P. (1998). *The courage to teach: Exploring the inner landscape of a teacher's life.* San Francisco: Jossey-Bass.

Phelan, A. M. (2005). On discernment: The wisdom of practice and the practice of wisdom in teacher education. In G. F. Hoban (Ed.), *The missing links in teacher education design: Developing a multi-linked conceptual framework* (pp. 57–73). Dordrecht, The Netherlands: Springer.

Schön, D. A. (1983). *The reflective practitioner: How professionals think in action.* New York: Basic Books.

Shapiro, D. H. Jr., and Walsh, R. N. (Eds). (1984). *Meditation: Classic and contemporary perspectives.* New York: Aldine.

Shapiro, S. L., and Carlson, L. E. (2009). *The art and science of mindfulness: Integrating mindfulness into psychology and the helping professions.* Washington, DC: American Psychological Association.

Shulman, L. S. (2004). *The wisdom of practice: Essays on teaching, learning, and learning to teach.* San Francisco: Jossey-Bass.

Siegel, D. J. (2007). *The mindful brain: Reflection and attunement in the cultivation of well-being.* New York: W. W. Norton & Company.

Smalley, S. L., and Winston, D. (2010). *Fully present: The science, art, and practice of mindfulness*. Philadelphia, PA: Da Capo Press.

Varela, F. J. (1999). *Ethical know-how: Action, wisdom, and cognition*. Stanford, CA: Stanford University Press.

Wansink, B. (2006). *Mindless eating: Why we eat more than we think*. New York: Bantam Books.

Young, J., Levin, B., & Wallin, D. (2007). *Understanding Canadian schools¨An introduction to educational administration* (4th ed.). Toronto: Nelson.

TWO

Critical Friends

The Practiced Wisdom of Professional Development

Karen Ragoonaden and Shawn Michael Bullock

As Shawn and I began our journey as critical friends, I shared a poem that I had written about Joseph Dunne, a visiting scholar on my campus who wrote the great philosophical treatise *Back to the Rough Ground* (1993). The purpose of this volume was to inquire about educators' conceptions of pedagogy and to explore implications for the relationship between theory and practice in Teacher Education Programs. Dunne's work was dense, rich, and profound. By writing the poem, I was able to deconstruct epistemological abstractions, progress towards new knowledge and to clarify understandings and tensions not only in my own practice but in my practices outside my own.

> In Nicomachean Ethics, a sage patrician reflected on techne and phronesis,
> Considering them to be two modes of knowledge,
> Recognized as Productive and Practical knowledge,
> Techne is defined as expert knowledge in one of specialized crafts,
> Whereas, Phronesis flowing from the practical knowledge of praxis,
> Recognizes the universal ideas of moral knowledge like justice and equity,
>
> In post-modern paradigms, where to situate techne and phronesis?
> Lured into a technical orientation that promises objectivity and predictability, it seems that the rationalization of teaching impedes wise judgements

Addressing teaching as an activity based in techne where has practical
wisdom gone?
Phronesis, acknowledging the complexity of human relationships, the
intuitive perception of teaching and the cultivation of imagination,
triumphs technique

And thus, the sage's complex, abstract conceptions offer the seductive
promise of abandoning the lure of technique to embrace the dynamic
complexity of practice and praxis, that is practical wisdom.

Reflecting on our own progression beyond the lure of technique towards
the dynamic complexity of practical wisdom, Shawn and I, as critical
friends and despite geographical distances, embarked on an on-line collaborative self-study. While recognizing the importance of *techne* in this
endeavour, we also searched for a substantive process that would awak-
en and entice our conceptions of *phronesis* (practical and moral knowledge) in our own professional development. Initially, we felt that critical
friendship would help us to understand specific features of our practice.
We would soon discover, though, that a commitment to the process of
being critical friends requires commitment to moving in unanticipated
directions.

As we meandered through the challenges in the miasma of technological facilitation for our collaborative work at a distance, we were often
surprised at what we discovered. To begin with, we asked ourselves:
How does a critical friendship develop across geographical distance?
How do we, as teacher educators use technology to facilitate shared narratives and constructive feedback? We learned that a systemic approach
to critical friendship is a process in which teachers interrogate the complexity of practice, invoke discussions about educational reform, and ulti-
mately transform the scholarship of teaching and learning. John Dewey
(1938) called for teachers to engage in *reflective action* and Donald Schön
(1983, 1987) depicted professional practice as a cognitive process of framing and exploring problems identified by educators for educators. We
did note the tradition of teachers asking their own questions and discerning patterns that are not always observed by others (Fichtman Dana and
Yendol-Hoppey, 2009). In fact, Cochran-Smith and Lytle (1999) address
the various efforts of progressive educators to construct alternative ways
to approach teaching and learning and argue that the traditional knowledge base for teaching failed to account for the knowledge generated by
educators. In keeping with the importance of multiple perspectives, Samaras (2011), taking her cue from Richardson (1994; 2000) characterizes
critical friends as *prisms* (p. 214) providing unique mindsets that inform
practice and praxis, which within the right context develop into rich data
sources. Schuck and Russell (2005) assert that the constructive tone of a
critical friend is essential in self-study. Since it is difficult to assess and
reframe one's practice, a critical friend nurtures the emergence of alter-

nate frames of reference upon which to introduce change. They state: "A critical friend acts as a sounding board, asks challenging questions, supports reframing of events, and joins in the professional learning experience" (p. 107). Costa and Kallick (1993) position critical friends within a paradigm where learning occurs via regular dialogue and regular feedback.

More recently, Hultman Özek, Edgren, and Jandér (2012) undertook a comprehensive literature review of the term *critical friend and peer observation* in order to learn about implementing the critical friend method in an academic library setting. This search indicated that a variety of definitions or statements of the term "critical friend" exists and that negative results are rarely published. For example, Swaffield (2007) refers to critical friend as a supportive yet challenging relationship between professionals, encouraging and cultivating constructive critique and requiring a knowledge of the context of the teaching environment. The literature concluded that the utilization of the critical friend method in various educational contexts yielded beneficial professional development outcomes for the educators involved in this process: increased confidence, confirmation of good practice, a sense of belonging to a collegial community, and breaking the sense of isolation in teaching assignments.

Based on the above, within a scholarly context, critical friends can promote renewal by commenting on each other's practice, by instigating pointed questions, by collecting data about their reflections, by analyzing the data relating to relevant literature, by revolutionizing practice based on new understandings and finally, by sharing and disseminating this new knowledge. However, acknowledging that the concept of *critique* is often equated with judgment and criticism, a critical friendship requires understanding as well as a formal process. Critical friendships, therefore, must be nurtured in a climate of trust, compassion, and empathy, encouraging analysis, integrity, and culminating with an advocacy for success, necessary conditions for the emergence of practical wisdom. In this chapter we explore a number of interwoven themes, including what we learned about critical friendship, what we learned about specific elements of our practice as teacher educators, and what our future questions are in need of exploration. We invite the reader to consider moments when we write together and moments when we write by ourselves, inviting the reader into our practice.

CRITICAL FRIENDS: SIMILARITIES WITHIN DIFFERENCES

As part of our exploration of critical friendship, we, Karen and Shawn, concede that we teach at two different institutions in the province of British Columbia, Canada, share a passion for teacher education and a commitment to make our tacit knowledge explicit through collaborative self-study. Previous work brought us together to explore and analyze the challenges and opportunities of framing teacher as "change agents" (Bullock and Ragoonaden, 2014). We soon realized that our shared interests, our different backgrounds and our border-crossings offered many opportunities for us to engage in a critical friendship (Costa and Kallick, 1993; Hultman Özek, Edgren, and Jandér, 2012; Schuck and Russell, 2005; Samaras, 2011). Karen is a second language education professor whose work focuses on critical pedagogy, curriculum development, and culturally relevant pedagogy. Shawn is a science and technology education professor with a background in physics and the history and philosophy of science whose work focuses on the role of reflective practice in science teacher education and the epistemological challenges of learning from experience.

Border-Crossing

Critical pedagogy provides a lens through which traditional educational practices can be renegotiated through careful examination of the multiple relationships of race, class, and gender in schools and in society, (Ball and Tyson, 2011). In particular, Kanpol (1992) posits that emancipatory and libratory practices emanating from the concept of *similarities with differences,* that is the relation between ideologies, and the material configurations of race, class, and gender (p. 272) can promote democratic visions of education. Notwithstanding the concept of *similarities within differences* the theme of border-crossing resonates with our explorations into professional development Giroux (1992) defines border-crossing as

> Challenging, re-mapping, and renegotiating those boundaries of knowledge that claim the status of master narratives, fixed identities, and an objective representation of reality . . . (and) recognizing the situated nature of knowledge, . . . and the shifting, multiple and often contradictory nature of identity. (p. 26)

Border-crossing provides an interesting set of lenses that we can use to both reveal our prior assumptions and to encourage one another to come to see our practices differently, including: a rural/urban divide in the location of our institutions, different cognate disciplines in education (French and Physics), the perspectives afforded by our different genders and cultural backgrounds, and the foci of our research programs.

Metaphors

There are good reasons why many self-study researchers use metaphor as an analytic tool. Visser-Wijnveen, Van Driel, Van der Rijst, Verloop, and Visser (2009) used metaphors to examine academics' perceptions of research, knowledge, and teaching because of the potential for metaphors to "say what is actually meant but is difficult to explain" (p. 675). Significantly, they found that academics' metaphorical conceptions of research was weakly linked to their conceptions of teaching—a finding that points to the valuable role self-study for education professors interested in researching their own teaching. Hamilton (2004) used the metaphor of a cartographer as a way of charting the ways in which self-study methodology had contributed to the knowledge base on teacher education. Hamilton's work deals with the nature of knowledge in self-study, among other important questions, arguing in part that the warrant in self-study "seems to be based on trustworthiness, integrity, and solid research methodology rather than the more formal approaches taken by the more conventional researchers" (p. 384). Drawing from the tradition of metaphor in self-study research, Shawn suggested that Jasman's (2010) work on metaphors provided an illustrative case of the utility of considering border-crossing experiences that could be used in our study. Drawing on work from Giroux's (1992) seminal work, *Border crossings: Cultural workers and the politics of education* and Elbaz-Luwisch's (2001) focus exploring border pedagogy through storytelling, Jasman selected outcomes from five research projects completed over her career as data for a meta-analysis of her professional learning journey. As an experienced educator, Jasman argues that she developed new personal practical and professional knowledge as a result of re-considering her prior work in light of self-study and the metaphors of border-crossing (Clandinin and Connelly, 1995). Significantly, Jasman articulated six metaphors that we both found stimulating for analysis of our own work. Each metaphor is a reminder that "professional learning . . . can also be shaped by the way in which the traveller [self-study researcher] engages in the journey," as a *tourist, migrant, reluctant traveler, tour guide, trekker,* or *explorer* (p. 321). In particular, the metaphor of travel agent or tour guide resonated with both of us because it was representative of the many border-crossings that we had experienced in our evolving critical friendship.

> *Travel agent or tour guide: . . .* teachers who open their doors to others or arrange for learning journeys in their own territories so that others can become border-crossers and engage in professional learning through understanding of another''s personal practical knowledge or professional knowledge context. (Jasman, 2010 p. 321)

In many ways, anyone who engages in a collaborative self-study with a critical friend is a metaphorical *travel agent* or *tour guide* since part of the process involves crossing geographical, institutional, gendered, cultural and linguistic borders to explicate and to challenge pedagogical conceptions of teacher education. Further, we were motivated to look beyond the technical aspect (*techne*) of teaching in order to reflect on the complexity of our own shared practical wisdom (*phronesis*). Likewise, Macintyre Latta and Buck (2007) reinforce the tradition of self-study of teacher education practices as self-understandings of the nature of teaching in order to improve practice. They posit that "self-study is . . . key to professional development and reflects our desire to do more than "deliver" courses in teacher education" (p. 189).

With due consideration to the discussion surrounding border-crossings, metaphors, and professional development, our critical friendship was reframed around the following research question:

> How does Jasman's (2010) metaphor of border-crossing as a travel agent or tour guide explicate and/or challenge our conceptions of teacher education and inform our critical friendship as professional development?

The Process of Critical Friendship

Our critical friendship emphasized a shared, grounded reflective approach that generated feedback and an awareness of a deeper comprehension of the experience. Although we took Costa and Kallick's (1993) suggestion that we advocate for each other's work to heart, work by Samaras (2011) provided a clearer roadmap for our overarching self-study process, in particular that self-study should be a *personal situated inquiry* and a *systematic research process*, which includes opportunities to share new knowledge with colleagues. We particularly found Samaras' comments about sharing control over the feedback process to be helpful in framing our work.

We also believe it is important for critical friends to be aware of how their roles may shift during the collaborative self-study process. Although the focus of a particular conversation one week might be on, say, Karen's experiences, that does not necessarily mean that Shawn must solely play the role of interlocutor. In other words, there is an improvisational element to our critical friendship that relies on well-articulated improvisational theatre (or *improv*) principles such as saying "Yes" to a premise established by a partner, before finding ways to add to it (Johnstone, 1979). It may seem strange initially to equate critical friendship with improv, but they share a core premise: A good improviser accepts what a partner "offers on stage"—it is not up to her or him to suggest a new direction to a scene or to "take over" the scene. One must leave a formal agenda behind and focus on being in the moment with a partner or partners. Improvisational theatre requires a commitment to spontaneity, which in part means trusting a scene partner to accept a premise that you offer because you share a mutual that is larger than either of you individually (see Bullock 2014 for a further comparison between improv and self-study). To return to our example, then, Karen's experiences might serve as a starting point for examining Shawn's experiences, it might be "an offer" for Shawn to begin further investigation and discussion into his practice. Shawn may build on Karen's offer, (similar to the

"Yes, and . . ." principle in improvisational theatre), and together we build a shared dialog. This approach helps to reduce the chances of a collaborative self-study becoming too one-sided, or to much like a more traditional research interview.

METHODS

In keeping with the personal situated inquiry, the authors met once a month via Skype during the Fall 2013 semester for approximately one hour to describe and discuss the context, issues, challenges and successes arising from their teaching.

Sources of data for this study were research journals, analytic memos, and notes (Charmaz, 2006; Creswell, 2007) kept about each of our conversations as well as individualized reflections about our teaching practice: a first year course for Aboriginal Access students (Karen) and a graduate course in Education (Shawn). Audio recordings from the Skype meetings were analyzed to remind ourselves of particularly meaningful moments in our conversations and, when appropriate, transcribed to provide additional data. Often, we would write longer reflective narratives about our teaching experiences, the connections or lack of connections made with the content and/or students. The meetings were less about collecting data and more about creating a space for each of us to think aloud about our educational experiences and invite our critical friend to comment on problems of practice we might be experiencing. This was reflective of a critical collaborative inquiry where the critical friend asks questions to understand the practice and to clarify the context of teaching and learning. We were, also, mindful of the foci on a transparent and systematic research process required for self-study research (Pinnegar and Hamilton, 2009; Samaras, 2011) and of the guidelines for quality in autobiographical self-study research (Bullough and Pinnegar, 2001). Perspectives on tensions articulated in Berry (2007) and in Samaras (2011) shed additional light on our primary method of analysis—finding elements in the data that were examples of border-crossings as represented by the metaphor of travel agent or tour guide articulated by Jasman (2010). With the aim of generating new knowledge, we present our data in a way that invites the reader to travel through each of the author's reflections on our pedagogical development and our conversations during the academic year.

Systematic Research Process

Using a creative technique to collect data and to ensure validity, the analytic approach called crystallization (Ellingson, 2009; Richardson, 1994; 2000; Samaras, 2011) was utilized. Since self-study researchers use a multiplicity of methods to gather data (in our case: transcription of Skype meetings, research notes, narratives, memos, emails), the multiple dimensions and diversity of angles, like the prisms of a crystal, can lead to a deeper and more profound understanding of the research being conducted. The critical friendship process established by Costa and Kallick (1993) and Samaras (2011) were used as categories to present the results of the study: personal inquiry stance, critical collaborative inquiry, improved learning, systematic research, knowledge generation, and presentation. Jasman's description of the travel agent/tour guide as border-crossers engaging in professional learning provided the authors with a parameter within which to frame their research. Data collected from the Skype conversations, the research notes, analytic memos, and narratives provided a solid foundation upon which to connect ideas, develop reflective stances, and to determine inherent tensions and complexities of practice. As we read our data, we searched for the manifestation of similar notions and views with Jasman's metaphor of travel agent or tour guide. Samaras (2011) refers to this as check coding, wherein two coders work individually to establish similar or contrasting themes. Looking for patterns and recurring themes, we were able to identify two emergent themes relating to culturally relevant pedagogy in practice and the relational approach of digital technology on theory and practice. During the course of on-going multiple readings, these categories were related to the initial code of travel agent and tour guide. Both authors used extracts from research notes, memos, and emails to identify and to support the similarities and the differences of their experiences. For example, the following excerpt from Karen's journal states that:

> Today, Shawn and I talked about the challenge of using culturally relevant pedagogy in higher education. We discussed his experience with his graduate class and my experiences with my first year Access students. Both of us try hard to stay away from deficit theories however, often the conversation in class steer towards bias and discrimination (September, 2013).

Summarizing the information coming from the initial and the ensuing codification, we were able to construct our writing by juxtaposing practice (*techne*) with the emergence of *practical wisdom* (*phronesis*). Positioning this new knowledge as professional development, the following narratives offer summative insights into our journeys as critical friends. Each step of the process has been identified using the Critical Friend process established by Costa and Kallick (1993) and Samaras (2011).

CRITICAL PEDAGOGY: TRAVELING THROUGH KAREN'S PROFESSIONAL PRACTICE

Acknowledging the concept of border-crossing juxtaposed with the metaphor of the *travel agent or tour guide*, I (Karen) begin my collaborative self-study reflecting upon the content of my many Skype conversations with my critical friend, Shawn. I recognized that my foci based on the rural/urban divide of our professional practice, different cognate disciplines, and the diversity in our gender as well as socio-cultural backgrounds often colored the nature of our bilateral dialogues. In keeping with Jasman's (2010) reference, during these critical conversations, I was able to articulate my thoughts and concerns clearly and concisely, theorize about my professional practice, and engage in conversation with a colleague who challenged and explored my practice and praxis. Having just finished writing a chapter (Ragoonaden, 2014) on the impact of critical pedagogy on stalwart, traditional conceptions of teaching and learning, my mind was swirling with ideas relating to equity and parity in marginalized student populations in higher education.

Personal Inquiry Stance

Recognizing that critical pedagogy provides a conceptualization through which traditional educational paradigms can be dissected, molded, and shaped (Egbo, 2005; 2009; Kanpol, 1999; Kanpol and McLaren, 1995), I chose to explore my experience teaching a first year developmental course aimed at Aboriginal Access students through a collaborative self-study. EDUC 104 *Introduction to Academic Pedagogy: An Aboriginal Perspective* was representative of two years of hard work, applying for grants for curriculum development, indigenizing the content of the course, collaborating with institutional and community partners, and finally seeking senate, faculty, and departmental approval from the various pillars of university administration. Conceptualized as an experiment with Aboriginal and non-Aboriginal epistemological and theoretical approaches, the EDUC 104 course is based on the nationally recognized University 101 program developed by the University of Southern Carolina (Barefoot, 1993; Gardner, 1980, 1981). In keeping with research supporting a move away from a fragmented, linear paradigm commonly seen in Eurocentric educational systems, the pedagogy in EDUC 104 represented a progression towards a holistic pedagogy emphasizing interconnectivity with all aspects of the self (emotional, intellectual, physical and spiritual). My journal emphasizes the embodied teaching and learning that I was experiencing while recognizing the disconnect felt by some of my students:

Based on the time requirements to develop this innovative course steeped in establishing balance between the four aspects of the self, my practice should have been dynamic and energized. However, the reality of teaching this course was taking its toll on me-the four aspects of my Self were definitely unbalanced. To begin with, first-year students are not like post-graduate education students! Lacking any sense of professional decorum they arrived late to class: sometimes sixty minutes late for a ninety-minute class. Assignments were completed by approximately twenty five percent of the class despite numerous in-class reminders, bulk and personal e-mails, and interventions by peer mentors and Aboriginal Programs and Services. Absenteeism was endemic. Halfway through the semester, I was faced with the harsh reality that one third of this class was failing. The majority of my students were, without a doubt, experiencing in a visceral manner, a disembodiment, a true disconnect between the course content and their lives (October, 2013).

Collaborative Critical Inquiry

Acknowledging that Indigenous scholars are wary of conventional Western school structure (Armstrong, 2005; Claypool and Preston, 2011), I clarified with Shawn how I strove to adapt my pedagogy to the Aboriginal Medicine Wheel of Learning, an integral component of this course. Since indigenizing knowledge is recognized as an educational remedy empowering Aboriginal students, EDUC 104 *Academic Pedagogy: An Aboriginal Perspective* was designed to reflect epistemology emphasizing interconnectivity, where all facets of learning relate to one another on emotional, spiritual, mental, and physical levels. By applying precepts of the Medicine Wheel as outlined in *The Sacred Tree* (Bopp et al., 2004) to the cycle of learning, this developmental course should have been providing an opportunity for Access students to appropriate academic skills in a culturally relevant manner. In this way, students could apply their cultural background to the acquisition of new knowledge and skills development. This assimilation of new life and scholastic skills would, in theory, translate to a successful university experience leading to retention and degree completion.

Yet as I recounted to my critical friend, using the Medicine Wheel of Learning as a pedagogical approach was a challenging and complex enterprise. For example, I wondered:

> How do I make content from the textbook, in accordance with the Wheel of Medicine, flow in a circular manner? How does one teach the Cornell Method of note-taking, Muscle Reading Strategies, and critical writing while taking the emotional, physical, spiritual and intellectual self into consideration (September, 2013)?

I told Shawn that prior to every class, I came back to the important consideration of *interconnectivity*, and the fact that Aboriginal worldviews were important discourses aimed at fostering academic success for First Nations Peoples (Claypool and Preston, 2011). I had developed, in collaboration with institutional and community partners, a unique, innovative course which should be promoting the development of foundational academic skills thus ensuring a successful pathway for Aboriginal Access students. Peer mentors, the presence of Elders and holistic assessment practices were integral components of this course. However, only a small percentage of my students were responding to the indigenization of curriculum. As I reflected on this dire state of affairs and vocalized my concerns with my critical friend, I came back to my own practical wisdom: bridging theory and experience by acknowledging the disconnect between underrepresented students and Eurocentric practices of mainstream schooling in postsecondary institutions (Armstrong, 2005; Claypool and Preston, 2011).

Border-Crossing

Coming back to Jasman's (2010) metaphor of border-crossing, I recognized that my role in this class was one of the travel agent/tour guide. As a non-Aboriginal, my lived and professional experiences were very different to the harsh realities of the Access students I was teaching. Through conversations, I realized that many of these first year students, some far from heart and hearth, suffered from anxiety and loneliness. Economic woes and an endemic sense of otherness and marginalization further exacerbated the challenges they faced. Delving into my personal life history (Cole and Knowles, 1995; Heilman, 2000), I sought out a connection, an affinity that could provide a foundation upon which to understand implicitly the circuitous path of the Wheel of Medicine. Could I establish a connection and an empathetic understanding with students through a holistic, interconnected approach to teaching? As I progressed through my torturous journey, I also recognized that I had embroiled my urbanized colleague into a world of unrivaled first year experiences. In that respect, my critical friend, joined me en route as I adopted the persona of the travel agent/tour guide. From our privileged positions, our conversations reflected the nexus of my frustration and disappointment. I knew instinctively that I was not seeking any resolution to my dilemma. Rather, I was meandering through the dark woods negotiating the enlightened path of Aboriginal versus Non-Aboriginal principles of teaching and learning. The richness of our professional conversations and ensuing embodied practice, allowed me to delve deeper into the praxis surrounding my pedagogy.

As I revise the course for a September delivery, the act of articulating the joy of success on an emotional level, and the frustration of loss on an intellectual level, combined with the freedom to reflect on course revisions has paved the way towards a deeply satisfying professional development. This journey as a travel agent/tour guide has allowed me to experience the act of teaching on a visceral, embodied level exploring how emotion, intellect, physicality and spirituality interconnect and dissect. Using the Medicine Wheel of Learning as a guide juxtaposed with critical conversations has provided me with the clarity of mind to make sound revisions and culturally relevant decisions, which, hopefully, will impact positively on my students and my practice. This is an example of the journey I took on my path towards my own hard-earned practical wisdom.

DIGITAL TECHNOLOGIES: TRAVELING THROUGH SHAWN'S PROFESSIONAL PRACTICE

This collaborative self-study framed through critical friendship occurred during my first opportunity to teach in the graduate program at my current institution. My previous experience in teaching graduate courses at my former institution was, broadly speaking, framed around the intersections between adult education and digital technologies. I had always been somewhat uncomfortable with this literature because I felt there was a tendency to focus on either skill development or enthusiastic calls for technology-led reform in the field. Both foci felt as though they were not sufficiently engaged with the social, relational elements of how people actually used technology. Working with Karen enabled me to think about how these concerns about my field might stimulate a different way of working with graduate students.

Personal Inquiry Stance

By nearly any metric, most people would consider me (Shawn) to be a "technology enthusiast." I spent countless hours as a K–12 student teaching myself how to program in BASIC and learning about the technological underpinnings of the fledging Bulletin Board System (BBS) movement. A cherished childhood gift was a modem that allowed me to connect with newsgroups and to exchange email with friends near and far, in a manner that seemed like magic at the time. To this day, I make a point of spending a considerable amount of my personal time remaining up-to-date with developments in the tech industry. I routinely switch between five different operating systems in my personal and professional life—partly for pleasure and partly for pragmatic reasons—and I have lost many an hour down the rabbit hole of trying to make an old piece of technology conform to my wishes. I delight in tinkering with hardware and software. I took Edward Snowden's (Greenwald, 2013) revelations about widespread telephone and Internet surveillance somewhat personally, as I now realize that my personal belief in both the power of an open-access Internet and the importance of digital privacy ran deeper than I originally realized.

Despite this over-arching enthusiasm, I believe that I have a healthy skepticism about the educational potential of digital tools. I find claims about the revolutionary potential of new technologies both tiresome and humorous; the history of physics and technology reminds me that such claims have been made before—including with the widespread adoption of the chalkboard in the training of physicists at Cambridge (Warwick, 2003). Cuban (1986) also provides a sobering, yet accurate, analysis of the revolutionary claims about educational radio and television. I share Selwyn's (2011) concern that research on the use of technology in education has tended to be overly optimistic, lacking a solid grounding in theory, and at times dangerously close to replicating existing power structures within the educational system.

Border-Crossing

Collaborating with Karen in self-study helped me to clarify that my personal stance toward the use of digital technology informed, and was informed by, the stance that I take as someone in the field of education and technology. I recognized that the problems that tend to attract most of my academic attention in education and technology are not problems that are concerned with how technology might be implemented in classrooms, but a more of an ontological and sociological concern of how technologies are used for educational experiences inside and outside of classroom environments. Following a conversation with Karen, I asked myself "What are our responsibilities, where is the logic?" following a comment about the "juxtaposition of the personal and the professional" (November 1, 2013). I have long been concerned that my natural interest in technology might make me seem like a "tech booster"—indeed I have noticed anecdotally that many seem to assume that those of us who write about education and technology have an agenda of ensuring that the latest devices end up in the hands of teachers and students. Working with Karen helped me to realize that my personal inquiry stance was something that needed to be more clearly articulated. When I wrote about my "responsibilities" as an academic and the "logic" of how my personal and professional relationships with digital technologies are connected, I was, in fact, scolding myself. Karen helped my to realize that the practical wisdom I have developed over a lifetime of pushing technologies to their limits in my personal life gives me a warrant for bringing my personal concerns into my academic line of inquiry. I am somewhat embarrassed by this revelation, as my academic background in technology has focused on the history of technology. For some reason, though, I was somewhat unwilling to bring my personal life history into my consideration of the role of technology in education. I credit my work with Karen

for helping me conceptualize a new line of research into the role of privacy in technology and education, motivated by a more clearly articulated
personal inquiry stance.

Critical Collaborative Inquiry: A Relational Approach to Using Digital
Technologies

My work with Karen has helped me to re-visit and expand upon an
idea that I (Shawn) first mentioned in Bullock (2011) when I became
interested in the use of blogs to extend and develop the relationship
between teacher candidates and their teacher educator. This self-study
has stimulated further thought on what I call, following Kitchen's (2005)
work, *a relational approach to using digital technologies*. A considerable
amount of the literature in digital technologies in education seems to
focus either on acquiring technical skills for the use of technology in
particular contexts and the related challenges of adoption and diffusion,
or the ways in which people use technology to accomplish particular
learning tasks. Both of these sets of literature are important, but I have
recently become far more interested in what Desjardins, Lacasse, and
Bélair (2005) referred to as the social competencies associated with using
digital technologies. Our conversations caused me to reframe how I think
about technology, particularly the extent to which I take the social affor-
dances of technology for granted when I have not *specifically* set up a
situation in which I believe technology is serving a social purpose (as in
the case of my use of blogs). Karen captured the ethos of the social capital
that even the common technology of voice-over-internet programs
(VOIP) such as Skype provide:

> Minutes prior to Skype meetings, I was often rushed, stressed and in
> the middle of an academic and/administrative deadline with col-
> leagues and/or students hammering at my office door! However, de-
> spite this anxiety-laden context, the pre-ordained meetings with my
> distanced colleague had a calming effect on me. I would firmly shut the
> door on the chaos, and await Shawn's hearty greeting, smiling face and
> calm demeanor, albeit via a computer screen. Once I entered this zone
> of critical confidentiality, I experienced a transformative process simi-
> lar to a *savasana* (yoga pose culminating in the union of the mind and
> the body). Jasman (2010) refers to this as a type of professional learning
> as an experience that is shaped and molded by the embodied journey
> of the self-study researcher (November, 2013).

In one of our conversations, I casually remarked to Karen that our self-
study does not seem to have much to do with technology—which initially was going to be one of our foci for study—because most of our conversations tended to focus on the challenges we were having with enacting
pedagogies in unfamiliar teaching situations. Karen gently pointed out
that the enormous relief that we both felt knowing that we had set aside

time to talk about our teaching with a trusted colleague would not have been possible without telephone technology at the very least and, as Karen's comments highlight above, the addition of video allowed us to both attend to the non-verbal signals that are regular features of communication. This realization was particularly important (and ironic) given my earlier critique of the tendency to focus on technical rather than social competencies for using digital technologies.

REFRAMING OUR UNDERSTANDINGS OF PEDAGOGY: BORDER-CROSSING AND METAPHORS

Improved Learning

Reflecting on the previous narratives, we acquiesce that the dominant metaphor in our early work is that of *travel agent or tour guide*, defined by Jasman (2010) as one who "arranges for learning journeys in their own territories so that others can become border-crossers and engage in professional learning through understanding of another's personal practical knowledge or professional knowledge context" (p. 321). Karen acted as a tour guide for Shawn as she shared the problems she encountered adapting culturally relevant pedagogy into a new course. This often led to conversations focusing on identity, integrity and cultural discontinuities present in both our normative institutionalized practices at an urban university and at a rural university. For example, Ogbu (1982; 1990) hypothesizes that unexamined cultures of learning may lead to cultural discontinuities and hinder the learning and emotional well-being of students. He labels these differences in found primarily in schooling as inherently discontinuous with the home and community experiences of learners. So, cultural discontinuities as theorized by Ogbu (1982; 1990) may explain the disconnect Aboriginal Access students experienced when they encountered a non-Aboriginal instructor using metaphors from the Wheel of Medicine to teach developmental skills necessary for academic success. This realization came to fruition in a progressive, cumulative manner during the span of Skype conversations during the course and after the course. This unfolding and unearthing of practical wisdom was fueled by the critical interactions between two colleagues who sought out challenging narratives in an attempt to perfect practice.

Recognizing the fluidity of identity and culture, in a moment of reframing, Shawn realized how his previously unexamined experiences as a student with special needs in the K–12 system have had his views of classes designed for specific groups of students. He was surprised to realize that he had never before explicitly considered his experiences as a K–12 student with special needs as a source for prior assumptions about teaching and learning. This moment of insight, obtained through Karen's discussion of her teaching experiences, demands further self-study of Shawn's practice Similarly, Shawn acted as a tour guide for Karen giving her the space and freedom to express to interrogate, to examine and to consciously analyze attributes of her practice. Our work provides further evidence of the power of collaborative self-study for, in the words of Kearney (2004), experiencing ourselves through the eyes of another. These experiences are particularly germane when we cross borders in our research and our practice into new ways of thinking about pedagogy. As Cochran-Smith and Lytle (1999) suggest practitioner inquiry generating new knowledge must be examined within the discourse and terminology of education.

Acknowledging Kearney's (2004) and Cochran-Smith and Lytle's (1999) perspective, educators should be required to critique all aspects of their professional and academic work. In the same way that peer review is a central tenet to the promotion and tenure process in academia, then critical self-reflection should be an integral component of teacher educators' and teacher researchers' praxis. Critical pedagogues (Ball and Tyson, 2011; Egbo, 2005, 2009; Nieto, 2000) recommend that educators, whether they be of scholastic or practitioner ilk, should be given opportunities to reflect on identity and privilege. This type of critical consciousness involves interrogating the multiple, complex identities of the self while interrupting mainstream ideological discourses which reinforce the reproduction of normative curricular and assessment practices. Educators who demonstrate critical consciousness can then begin to question their own positions, assumptions, and beliefs about themselves and values that impact teaching.

Knowledge Generation and Presentation

In keeping with the focus on developing criticality in a progressive scaffolding of ideas, concepts and epistemologies, our critical friendship builds upon previous experience through reflection and revision facilitating and promoting transformative pedagogy and practice. By reflecting on significant professional events and analyzing these circumstances, teacher educators can focus on developing successful strategies which explore pathways between practice and praxis, in Dunne's (1993) words, *techne* and *phronesis*, particularly in non-traditional educational contexts. Loughran (2014) recognizes that teacher educators' professional development needs to be navigated without "limiting the journey to one single 'true' or correct path" (p. 2). This exploration is perfectly positioned within Jasman's (2010) conceptualization of metaphors, particularly as travel agent or tour guide, to describing the professional learning and development of teacher educators. This access to a metaphorical journey provided both of us with the necessary parameters to explore and examine our own practical wisdom through practice and praxis. Collaborative self-study coupled with critical friendship proved to be a rite of passage in our professional development allowing us to connect critically and creatively with a like-minded colleague. This is indeed a rare occurrence.

CONCLUSIONS

We began our collaborative self-study with the "allure of technique," that is, we were initially focused on examining specific features of our own practices with a view to understanding more deeply, in the first case, Karen's approach to working with Aboriginal students and, in the second case, Shawn's use of technology in teaching his graduate students. What emerged, though, was a collaborative self-study that focused on the nature and scope of our critical friendship. We learned that, for the duration of this initial study, it was more important for us to understand the complex social and emotional dimensions of each other as critical friends rather than to focus on specific, more process-oriented questions about the practice of being critical friends. We certainly discussed some technical aspects of our teacher education practices, but we found that our critical friendship moved freely from technical domains to more relational ones. Allowing ourselves to freely respond to one another and to suggest lines of thinking that the other person might not have considered drew us away from the initial catalysts for our work, to some extent. Importantly, however, this same openness and willingness to share control over feedback allowed us to explore novel territory in our practices and to uncover tacit assumptions.

We have learned that critical friendship, when given space and time, emerges organically from the multiple strands of negotiated dialogue. Commensurate with Jasman's (2010) conceptualization of new professional knowledge, as well as the focus of Hultman Özek et al., (2012) on implementing the critical friendship method as a powerful tool to facilitate the process of continuous improvement in teaching, critical friendship can be framed as a type of professional development, shaped, and molded by the history of self-study researchers as they progress and as they engage in the examination of their practice (Macintyre and Buck, 2007). Much like Loughran's (2005; 2014) assertion that there is no one right way to do a self-study, the diverse dimensions of critical friendship in collaborative self-study work demonstrate that this type of supported inquiry is malleable and flexible enough to mold itself into to multiple contexts of professional development.

REFERENCES

Armstrong, J. (2005). Okanagan education for sustainable living: As natural as learning to walk or talk. In M. Stone and Z. Barlow (Eds.), *Ecological literacy: Educating our children for a sustainable world*. (pp. 80–84). San Francisco, CA: Sierra Club Books.

Ball, A., and Tyson, C. (Eds.). (2011). *Studying diversity in teacher education*. Lanham, MD: Rowman & Littlefield.

Barefoot, B. O. (Ed.). (1993). *Exploring the evidence: Reporting outcomes of freshman seminars* (Monograph No. 11). Columbia, SC: University of South Carolina, National Resource Center for The Freshman Year Experience.

Berry, A. (2007). Reconceptualizing teacher educator knowledge as tensions: Exploring the tension between valuing and reconstructing experience. *Studying Teacher Education* 3: 117–134.

Bopp, J., Bopp, M., Brown, L. and Lane, P. (2004). *The sacred tree*. Twin Lakes, WI: Lotus Press.

Bullock, S. M. (2011). Teaching 2.0: (Re)learning to teach online. *Interactive Technology and Smart Education* 8, no. 2: 94–105.

Bullock, S. M. (2014). Self-study, improvisational theatre, and the reflective turn: Using video data to challenge my pedagogy of science teacher education. *Educational Research for Social Change* 3, no. 2: 37–50.

Bullock, S. M. and Ragoonaden, K. (2014, May). *Critical friendship as critical pedagogy: Developing pedagogies of change through collaborative self-study*. Paper presented at the Canadian Society for Studies in Education Conference, St. Catharines, Ontario.

Bullough, R. V. Jr., and Pinnegar, S. (2001). Guidelines for quality in autobiographical forms of self-study research. *Educational Researcher* 30, no. 3: 13–21.

Charmaz, K. (2006). *Constructing grounded theory: A practical guide through qualitative analysis*. Los Angeles, CA: Sage.

Clandinin, D. J., and Connelly, F. M. (1995). *Teachers' professional knowledge landscapes*. New York: Teachers College Press.

Claypool, T. and Preston, J. (2011). Redefining learning and assessment practices impacting Aboriginal students: Considering Aboriginal priorities via Aboriginal and Western worldviews. *Indigenous Education* 17, no. 3: 84–95. Retrieved from: http://ineducation.ca/index.php/ineducation/article/view/74.

Cochran-Smith, M., and Lytle, S. (1999). Relationship of knowledge and practice: Teacher learning in communities. In A. Iran-Nejad and C. Pearson (Eds.), *Review of research in education* (Vol. 24, pp. 249–306) Washington, DC: American Educational Research Association.

Coles, A., and Knowles, G. (1995). Methods and issues in a life history approach to self- study. In T. Russell and F. Korthagen (Ells.), *Teachers who teach teachers: Reflections on teacher education* (p.130–51). London: Falmer.

Costa, A., and Kallick, B. (1993). Through the lens of a critical friend. *Educational Leadership* 51, no. 2: 49–51.

Creswell, J. W. (2007). *Qualitative inquiry and research design: Choosing among five approaches*. Thousand Oaks, CA: Sage.

Cuban, L. (1986). *Teachers and machines: The classroom use of technology since 1920*. New York: Teachers College Press.

Desjardins, F., Lacasse, R., and Bélair, L. (2001). Toward a definition of four orders of competency for the use of information and communication technology (ICT) in education. In *Proceedings of the IASTED International Conference on Computers and Advanced Technology in Education* (pp. 213–217). Banff, Canada: ACTA Press.

Dunne, J. (1993). *Back to the rough ground: Practical judgment and the lure of technique*. Notre Dame: University of Notre Dame Press.

Dewey, J. (1938). *Experience and education*. New York: Collier Books.

Egbo, B. (2005). Critical pedagogy as transformative micro-level praxis. AE-Extra. Retrieved from http://www.unco.edu/ae-extra/2005/6/Art-4.html

Egbo, B. (2009). *Teaching for diversity in Canadian schools.* Toronto: Pearson Education Canada.

Elbaz-Luwisch, F. (2001). Personal story as passport: storytelling in border pedagogy. *Teacher Education* 12, no. 1: 81–101.

Ellingson, L. L. (2009). *Engaging crystallization in qualitative research: An introduction.* Thousand Oaks, CA: Sage.

Fichtman Dana, N., and Yendol-Hoppey, D. (2009). *Teacher inquiry defined: The reflective educator's guide to classroom research.* Thousand Oaks, CA: Corwin Press.

Gardner, J. N. (1980). *University 101: A concept for improving teaching and learning.* Columbia, SC: University of South Carolina. (ERIC Reproduction Service No. 192 706).

Gardner, J. N. (1981). Developing faculty as facilitators and mentors. In V. A. Harren, M. N. Daniels and J. N. Buck (Eds.), *Facilitating students' career development* (pp. 67–80). New Directions for Student Services, No. 14. San Francisco: Jossey-Bass.

Giroux, H. (1992). *Border crossings: Cultural workers and the politics of education.* New York: Routledge.

Greenwald, G. (2013, June 6). NSA collecting phone records of millions of Verizon customers daily. *The Guardian.* Retrieved from http://www.theguardian.com/world/2013/jun/06/nsa-phone-records-verizon-court-order.

Hamilton, M. L. (2004). Professional knowledge, teacher education and self-study. In J. J. Loughran, M. L. Hamilton, V. K. LaBoskey, and T. Russell (Eds.), *International handbook of self-study of teaching and teacher education practices* (pp. 375–419). Dordrecht, The Netherlands: Springer.

Heilman, E. (2003). Critical theory as a personal project: From early idealism to academic realism. *Educational Theory* 53, no. 3: 247–74.

Hultman Özek, Y., Edgren, G., and Jandér, K. (2012). Implementing the critical friend method for peer feedback among teaching librarians in an academic setting. *Evidenced Based Library and Information Practice* 7, no. 4: 68–81.

Jasman, A. M. (2010). A teacher educator's professional learning journey and border pedagogy: A meta-analysis of five research projects. *Professional Development in Education* 36, no. 1: 307–23.

Johnstone, K. (1979). *Impro: Improvisation and the theatre.* New York: Routledge.

Kanpol, B. (1992). Postmodernism in education revisited: Similarities within differences and the democratic imaginary. *Educational Theory* 42, no. 2: 217–29.

Kanpol, B. (1999). *Critical pedagogy: An introduction.* Westport, CT: Bergin and Garvey.

Kanpol, B., and McLaren, P. (Eds.) (1995). *Critical multiculturalism: Uncommon voices in common struggle.* Westport, CT: Bergin and Garvey.

Kearney, R. (2004). *On stories.* London: Routledge.

Kitchen, J. (2005). Conveying respect and empathy: Becoming a relational teacher educator. *Studying Teacher Education* 1, no. 2: 195–207.

Loughran, J. (2005). Researching teaching about teaching: Self-study of teacher education practices. *Studying Teacher Education* 1, no. 1: 5–16.

Loughran, J. (2014). Professionally Developing as a Teacher Educator. *Journal of Teacher Education* 65, no. 4: 271–83

Macintyre Latta, M., and Buck, G. (2007) Professional Development Risks and Opportunities Embodied within Self-Study. *Studying Teacher Education: A journal of self-study of teacher education practices* 3, no. 2: 189–205

Nieto, S. (2000). Placing equity front and center: some thoughts on transforming teacher education for a new century. *Journal of Teacher Education* 51: 180–87.

Ogbu, J. U. (1982). Cultural discontinuities and schooling. *Anthropology & Education Quarterly* 13, no. 4, 290–307.

Ogbu, J. U. (1990). Minority status and literacy in comparative perspective. *Daedalus* 119, no. 2: 141–68.

Pinnegar, S., and Hamilton, M. L. (2009). *Self-study of practice as a genre of qualitative research.* Dordrecht: Springer.

Ragoonaden, K. (2014). Transformative praxis: Barry Kanpol and the quest for a public identity. In S. Totten and J. Pederson (Eds.), *Educating about social issues in the 20th and 21st centuries: Critical pedagogues and their pedagogical theories.* (Vol. 4, pp. 186–211). Charlotte, NC: Information Age Publishing.

Richardson, L. (1994). Writing: A method of inquiry. In N. K. Denzin and Y. S. Lincoln (Eds.), *Handbook of qualitative research* (pp. 516–29). Thousand Oaks, CA: Sage Publications.

Richardson, L. (2000). Writing: A method of inquiry. In N. K. Denzin and Y. S. Lincoln (Eds.), *Handbook of qualitative research* (2nd Ed. 923–48). Thousand Oaks, CA: Sage Publications.

Samaras, A. P. (2011). *Self-study teacher research: Improving your practice through collaborative inquiry.* Thousand Oaks, CA: Sage

Schön, D. (1983). *The reflective practitioner: How professionals think in action.* San Francisco: Jossey-Bass.

Schön, D. (1987). *Educating the reflective practitioner.* San Francisco: Jossey-Bass.

Schuck, S., and Russell, T. (2005). Self-study, critical friendship, and the complexities of teacher education. *Studying Teacher Education* 1, no. 2: 107–21.

Selwyn, N. (2011). Editorial: In praise of pessimism—the need for negativity in educational technology. *British Journal of Educational Technology* 42: 713–18.

Swaffield, S. (2007). Light touch critical friendship. *Improving Schools* 10, no. 3: 205–19. In Hultman Özek, Y., Edgren, G., and Jandér, K. (2012). Implementing the critical friend method for peer feedback among teaching librarians in an academic setting. *Evidenced Based Library and Information Practice* 7, no. 4: 68–81.

Visser-Wijnveen, G. J., Driel, J. H. V., Rijst, R. M. V. der, Verloop, N., and Visser, A. (2009). The relationship between academics' conceptions of knowledge, research and teaching—a metaphor study. *Teaching in Higher Education* 14, no. 6: 673–86.

Warwick, A. (2003). *Masters of theory: Cambridge and the rise of mathematical physics.* Chicago: The University of Chicago Press.

THREE

Critical Friendship as Mindful and Relational Professional Development

Leyton Schnellert and Pamela Richardson

Situating Ourselves

Over 10 years our lives and work have intersected in ways that integrate personal and professional development through a range of scholarly and social contexts. Across these contexts, we have been engaged in an extended conversation about social justice-oriented theory and practice in education. Three years ago we found ourselves in the same Faculty of Education as new faculty members. Soon after taking up our positions, a significant mindfulness initiative was launched in the faculty as a whole, as part of an overarching effort to reposition and brand the faculty. As scholar-practitioners who already took up mindfulness in our own scholarship and pedagogies (Schnellert, Richardson, and Cherkowski, 2014), we struggled to engage with a mindfulness discourse that did not espouse criticality and potentially even furthered a neo-liberal agenda based in individualistic approaches focused, for example, on stress reduction.

We arrived with our own intellectual and experiential understandings of mindfulness based in years of practice informed by our personal and professional commitments. Our understandings of what constitutes mindful pedagogic and research practices are based in responsive, participatory, and social justice-oriented praxis and inquiry. Our understanding of critical mindfulness underscores the complex experience of being in the world and values relational and critically engaged practices (Richardson, 2014; Schnellert, Kozak, and Moore, 2015). We draw on Greene's (1978) notion of "awakeness"; Meyer's (2010) practice of Living Inquiry

33

with a focus on the self/other dimension of experience; Noddings's (2002) notion of reciprocal care, which draws attention to the experience of both participants within the caring relation; and an awareness of how to work in "power-with" arrangements (see the work of Mary Parker Follett discussed in Kreisberg, 1992; Richardson, Cherkowski, and Schnellert, 2015). As this conversation around mindfulness within teacher education grew within and beyond our faculty, we sought to make visible those approaches and understandings of mindfulness resonant with critical pedagogy, diversity-positive mindsets, and situated inquiry practices (Malhotra-Bentz and Shapiro, 1998; Meyer, 2010; Moll, 2014; Stanley, 2012).

Our scholarship is predicated on the assumption that self and context are mutually constituted; if we step into certain practices, agendas, and structures, we risk embodying those practices and structures. We also make our path by walking (Varela, Thompson, and Rosch, 1991) and shape our contexts through our agency, voice, and influence. As critical friends (Berry and Russell, 2014; Samaras, 2011) who choose to walk significant parts of our professional paths together, we consciously negotiate what our steps might entail. As scholar-practitioners, we are learning professionals who consciously work to align our values, research, and teaching through self study of our practice. As we co-constructed this chapter, working at a distance, using diverse digital and online technologies, we continued to weave and co-construct what it means for us to be critical friends. We have lived, critiqued, dwelled with and inquired into the implications of our own embodiment (e.g., Richardson, 2014; Richardson, 2010) and contemplated the ethics held within particular choices and ways of being. As critical friends, we work to challenge, support, and influence each other towards transforming contexts and structures that discount non-dominant, diverse ways of being and knowing such as queer, feminist, arts-based and non-hierarchical epistemologies.

One of the challenges we encountered to our critical friendship was being split into various projects, roles, and contexts due to institutional demands. Also our pre-tenure, and at that point for Pamela contingent, faculty status gave us a relative lack of power to maintain and support our desired positions. This gave us less stable ground to work upon to take up critically-oriented, power-with positions within a power-over institution. Also, some of the roles and opportunities that we were swept into both together and individually clashed with our critically-minded, scholar-practitioner values, and so we sometimes struggled to work within and through the status-quos of our context. Thus, our critical friendship was essential to our ability to not only conceptualize, but also develop and extend our work within our teaching and research.

Self-Study and Critical Friendship

This piece is a self study into how we co-created critical spaces for our professional development within the larger, shifting context of our work. We offer two examples of how through critical friendship (Berry and Russell, 2014; Samaras, 2011) we negotiated the co-creation of critically mindful spaces and spaces for mindful inquiry. Malhotra-Bentz and Shapiro (1998) define mindful inquiry as "a creative act. It seeks not only to discover or to record what is there, but to allow what is there to manifest itself in a new way, to come forward in its "shining" (p. 54). In our self studies, collaborative writing features largely in our shared practice, and we infuse reflexive narrative inquiry methods—exploring, remembering, and conversing through writing (Schnellert and Butler, 2014). Etherington (2007) writes that collaborative narrative inquirers "may become actively involved in co-constructing previously untold stories by asking curious questions that help thicken and deepen existing stories and invite the teller into territory beyond what is already known to him or her" (p. 600). During this self study we surfaced questions such as: How are we both critical and mindful in our personal/professional relationship? How do we live mindfulness? How does critical mindfulness transform our relationship to the academy? How is mindfulness defined and used to encourage acceptance of practices and agendas that smooth away and discourage diversity, plurality, resistance and creativity? Clandinin, Pushor and Orr (2012) suggest that narrative inquirers "think of their inquiry phenomenon, topic, puzzle, and participants as occurring in a multidimensional, ever changing life space. To plan a narrative inquiry is to plan to be self-consciously aware of everything happening with that life space" (p. 481). For us, collaborative self study helps us to unpack events, experiences and how our critical friendship supports us to make spaces for social justice in our teaching, interactions with colleagues, and at the program level. Below we offer reflections, one authored by each of us (and refined and polished together), to illustrate our efforts to co-create spaces for mindful and critical pedagogy.

Pamela's Perspective

In the summer of 2012, when I joined the Faculty, Leyton had begun, along with the associate dean at the time, laying groundwork to change the design of the initial semester of our Secondary Teacher Education Program (STEP). Conversations about teacher education program renewal were being encouraged in our faculty. I was hired initially to support the development and launch of this new summer semester. Given this climate and interest in new possibilities, we worked, along with the larger summer instructional team, to re-conceptualize the semester as an intensive, interdisciplinary, inquiry-based, co-taught, seven-week course that wove together foundational knowledge in Education (Psychology, Sociology, Foundations, Literacy) through case-based inquiry and collaborative learning. Because of our previous experiences working collaboratively, as well as our shared pedagogical commitments and social justice orientations to teaching, the approach we devised was well aligned with our relational, situated, and critically-oriented understandings of what it means to develop as a professional educator (see Richardson et al., 2015a).

It is probably not surprising that not everyone on the instructional team was equally well aligned or on board with a new approach that featured interdisciplinarity, collaborative inquiry, situated, and relational epistemologies, and critical perspectives. There were, as could be expected, diverse and strong perspectives within our team of six, on how teacher education should unfold. Albeit collaboratively developed in parts, not everyone was equally committed to the vision and practice we were constructing. There was a range of positions from uncertain but still curious and willing, to vocally skeptical and resistant. Part of our shared work then was, for the benefit of the teacher candidates in our program, to engage mindfully with all six faculty who were to be part of this summer semester, and to include them in the vision as active contributors and creators. With this as the goal, we sought to facilitate a shared vision that welcomed diverse content areas, epistemological stances and practices within an intersecting pedagogical approach.

Core to the semester was our overlapping foci on collaborative inquiry, reflexivity, and social justice embedded within and across diverse case studies and disciplines. Teacher candidates would work collaboratively with assigned faculty members within mentor groups to inquire into and develop responses to six different cases, introduced week-by-week by different faculty who were content area experts in their discipline (e.g., human development; educational psychology; literacy etc.). Also from the outset, we wished to inquire into our shared practice and nurture a culture of practitioner inquiry, and so we co-engaged in a self study that involved the entire instructional team (Richardson et al., 2015b). By meeting weekly as part of our own inquiry project, and working together closely we were able to better echo, amplify, as well as complexify, one another's pedagogical positions and concepts. We were also able to model a productive co-teaching relationship for our B.Ed students as they observed us checking in with one another, referring to each other's concepts and practices, and collaboratively creating an emergent teaching and learning experience. Students also, though, witnessed the realities of a collaborative team where disjunctures and misalignments were sometimes present. We engaged authentically with tensions and shared some of this with students to invite them into the process of likewise grappling mindfully with their own relational realities within their collaborative inquiry groups. In this way, amongst others, we framed engaging mindfully with relationships in a collaborative setting as part of their emerging identity as a teaching professional.

When I reflect back over a number of years of shared practice what remains are less the sharp details and more the feeling tones and the deeper, embodied lessons. What I remember most about co-leading this semester with Leyton was a sense of connectedness and flow that enabled us to step forward visibly as co-leaders and enactors of a new vision in a skeptical faculty. The critical friendship that we developed became the linchpin that held the roller-coaster of an emergent collaborative process on track. Through collaborating we were able to be more courageous, creative, and clear about our intentions and better negotiate the pressures and intensity within the evolving situation.

I have only been on faculty for a few weeks. I have been hired into an instructor position and am at the beginning of a year long contract. The hope, I have been told, is that they will be able to create a permanent, tenure-track position for me. It is within this context, that I am stepping forward to lead the first case study within the first iteration of our newly revised summer semester. Everyone who is involved with the summer is in the room as I launch my first case. There is the group of 70 students newly arrived in their program, a small group of uncertain and even resistant faculty members who will be teaching their own case studies in the following weeks, the associate dean who supported the changes and who is part of the instructional team, and there is Leyton ready to support me from the sidelines. I am acutely aware that as the leader of the first case, beyond initiating the teacher candidates into the pedagogical process, and beyond modeling the approach for faculty, I am representing the worthiness of our emergent, inquiry-oriented approach and selling it to those more anxious members of our team. I feel nervous but not unclear or unsure of what I am doing. This first case study is focused on Adolescent Development, and I have decided to place relationship building and attachment at the center of the inquiry. What quickly becomes obvious to me as the week unfolds is not only that this first case study focuses on relationship building at the heart of teaching and learning, but that the relationships between faculty on the instructional team, between faculty and teacher candidates in their mentor groups, between the teacher candidates themselves, and between Leyton and I, serve as complex sites of learning that echo the core themes and theoretical orientations of the case. By engaging with these various relational sites in a reflexive manner, we are able to deepen and develop our practices of putting relationship mindfully at the center of teaching and learning.

In retrospect, a big part of what enabled me to make sense of this summer teaching together, was that I would often commute to work with Leyton and we would have a half hour many mornings and evenings where we could unpack the complexities of these layered sets of relationships. These conversations nurtured our own development as leaders, strengthened our own bonds of trust and affiliation around our work, and anchored our collaborative and relationally based pedagogy in our own relationship. It was through this critical friendship that we were able to sustain our commitment to our vision, continue to develop our practice, and model and extend our praxis. My critical friendship with Leyton nurtured my ability to teach Adolescent Development from an attachment based, relational perspective that first year of the revised program wherein I both reflected upon and nurtured attachments with and among my own teacher candidates. And, it was key to my ability to take a significant risk the second year and conceptualize a new case for week two of the summer, in which I approached human development from a critical perspective focused on adolescent sexuality, identity, media, and communication. While we supported teacher candidates to live generously and yet critically within their mentor groups, we were able to support one another as members of a complex instructional team where there were shared commitments to working together but varying degrees of comfort with the reflexive, interdisciplinary, emergent, inquiry-oriented pedagogy that we were proposing. In these ways, I witnessed the development of my own practice through the supportive relationship of a critical friend while putting relationality at the center of teacher candidates' learning about teaching.

Leyton's Perspective

After the first semester of our STEP, where faculty worked together to develop and realize an integrated co-taught semester, teacher candidates were expecting more of the same. However, the Fall semester involved six different courses including their pedagogical methods courses. This meant that they were never taught together as one large cohort and almost always grouped by specialty. Pamela and I found our opening to continue our self study and critical friendship by creating connections between our Fall courses. I taught *Middle School Integrated Methods* and *Assessment for Learning*. Pamela taught *English Language Arts Methods* and *Special Needs in Secondary Schools*.

Drawing on our experiences with narrative inquiry, we developed a practice of exploring "telling moments" from our practice (Fels and Belliveau, 2008; Routman, 2000; Schnellert et al., 2014). One of us identifies a telling moment—a moment of tension that burgeons with layers of meaning if we slow down and attend to it—and steps back to narrate it for the other. This typically involves taking time from the hectic pace of academic life to be present with one another, sharing themes we heard, posing questions, and suggesting possible interpretations. Writing up these telling moments makes our practice of self-study more accountable. We attend more deeply to events that we write about and unpack together. Through dwelling on emergent meanings and revisiting our commitments, we open to feedback that disrupts positions that do not align with our social justice oriented goals. What follows is a telling moment that Leyton shared with Pamela on a walk across campus to get tea.

"Leyton, can we schedule a conference with you?" Reena asked. She was one of my mentees that summer and now that the summer was over, I was thrilled that she still wanted to check in with me. I was feeling out of touch with my summer mentees who were not in my Middle specialty in the Fall. Over the summer we had invested a lot of time in building our individual and team relationships through conferencing and mentor group meetings. This was vital to me in supporting teacher candidates' individual and collaborative learning and informing my teaching. Now that it was Fall and STEP teacher candidates and courses were divided into subject areas. For the majority of the teacher candidates, especially those who were not in the middle school speciality and thus with me for three of their six courses, those relationships were potentially absent and/or diluted as they engaged in disparate courses and worked with a range of instructors.

At least Reena, one of my summer mentees, was in my assessment course. I'd noticed that she and another of the Humanities students, Lana, always sat together and had developed quite a connection. Reena had asked "Can we schedule a conference with you?" Was Lana hoping to connect, too?

"You and Lana?" I asked.

"No, all of the Humanities group," Reena replied.

Through her smile I sensed some tension. Why would all nine Humanities folks want a group conference? I looked calmly at Reena while my mind raced . . . What had I said in class? Was my pep rally passion for our Middle Methods classes seeping into my Assessment course?

In the Fall, I work to build a Middle School cohort based in community and taught in the community rather than at the university. We spend most of our time in schools throughout our region learning about teaching through teaching. By positioning the Middle school specialty as a very different option compared to the other STEP specialties, I worked to create pride and confidence in the path that was for most a second choice after they could not qualify for the Humanities cohort.

As I walked and talked with Pamela, trying to determine what might be behind the conference request, she asked me how the course was going, if the Humanities folks seemed engaged, and how they were doing with the 24 Middle: 9 Humanities ratio. Pamela knew me well enough to inquire if I was overcompensating on behalf of the Middles in the Assessment course.

By this time we were across campus and drinking our tea. Thanks to Pamela's prompting, I was able to recall that while all my Middles had participated in an optional school-based session in a local middle school to experience performance-based reading assessment, only one of the Humanities folks had come.

"How did you feel about that?" she asked.

"Disappointed and surprised," I shared. "But I just dove into the experience of modeling and facilitating the assessment process for the 30 grade nines and 25 teacher candidates."

The Humanities folks who had not been part of the experience joined us for our regular Monday afternoon class. Those who attended the session in the school described the process and then I led them through protocols for collaboratively assessing student work, setting goals, and making instructional plans based on what they had learned (Schnellert, Watson, and Widdess, 2015). Did the Humanities teacher candidates feel included or left behind? I didn't know if this was where the conversation with Reena and the rest of the Humanities group would go when we met, but talking with Pamela helped me think about potential power dynamics at play that I could ameliorate in terms of how my class was structured.

Before I met for a conference with the Humanities group, I checked in with Pamela again. I explained how I planned to surface what I thought was the issue and get their feedback. Pamela suggested that I let them lead rather than assume the exact nature of their concern. Pamela taught this same group their English methods course. She shared that her course was even more emergent and organic than anticipated. Meeting with Pamela a second time helped me to explore the relationship between our classes and let go of some of the control that I had taken in my effort to support the Middle cohort.

I met with the group after the next class. "How can I help?" I asked. The group was concerned that they would not be able to apply what I was teaching to secondary English because I had a Middle school slant. "How can I adjust my course?" I asked. The group mostly wanted to be heard and for me to know that they were worried. They did share that they felt like they had missed out on participating in the optional in situ assessment opportunity and that I needed to emphasize the importance of such events for those not also in my Middle Methods courses. We agreed that I would make more connections to high school Humanities in class and that I would collaborate with Pamela to (re)align our courses so that their unit plans and assessments were an opportunity to apply ideas between our courses. When I followed up with Pamela, she offered to co-plan and attend an assessment class and work with her Humanities group within the larger class. Pamela attended only one class, but the Humanities students felt heard and supported. The tone in my Assessment course changed as I more mindfully attended to the relationship between myself and the teacher candidates. I slowed down to draw in the voices and perspectives of everyone in the class making the learning richer for all.

One of the conditions that made for creative and powerful learning together was that, while we were not co-teaching teacher candidates as in the summer, we were able to build from this foundation. We were, for example, able to problem solve and plan how to integrate assessment within and across courses. By attending to this moment as critical friends we were able to align our teaching to reinforce ideas. Attending to this telling moment with the support of Pamela—stopping and reflecting on teacher candidates' and my experiences and actions—helped me as well as the students. This process allowed us to investigate tensions in our teaching (Berry and Russell, 2014) as Pamela and I negotiated our practice in relation.

Critical Friendship as Mindful and Relational Professional Development

Critically mindful friendship within self study is at the heart of how we have come to understand our professional development. It enables us to ground, embody, and co-author our identities through critically reflexive methods. In this section, we engage with critical questions we pose in order to reflect on the meaning and merit of our critical friendship in terms of supporting our professional development as mindful practitioners and scholars.

How are we both critical and mindful in our personal/professional relationship? How do we live mindfulness? How does critical mindfulness transform our relationship to the academy? How can critical mindfulness encourage acceptance of practices that encourage diversity, plurality, and change in the structures within which we work?

For us, these questions relate to our ability to enact social justice pedagogies and participatory and inclusive forms of inquiry. Self study has allowed us to iteratively check in and examine where our actions and intentions are aligning and/or coming apart. Like all work involving social change, it is incremental and non-linear. Through our conversations, we are able to step back and see the bigger picture and how social and organizational structures are barriers that we need to consider and address. We live our mindfulness through engaging in discussions that are difficult and through acknowledging and honoring the emotional and embodied nature of learning in relation. In both our narratives, we can see how we have sustained our efforts towards these goals through shared and intersecting work. Critically mindful professional development happens over time, in relation, moving back and forth between shared resonance, and offering vital lenses from outside our limited perspectives and lived experiences. Importantly, our work with students, staff and colleagues from across our campus who also take up critical theory has reinforced and extended our capacity to engage in intersectional analyses and related actions. This larger community of critical practice has helped us to grow beyond the limits of our paired frames of reference and supports us to further infuse critical mindfulness into work with one another. The way that we practice mindfulness welcomes others' frames of reference in order to recognize that there are no easy steps to dismantling power relations such as sexism, racism, classism, ableism, or homophobia in teaching, learning, and the institutions and communities that we work and live within. We have found intersections between the theories we take up with students, the pedagogy that we are developing, and our own personal/professional identity development.

When understood as a relational practice and process, critical mindfulness can be disruptive to academic cultures devoted to neoliberal agendas of individualism, competition, efficiency, and productivity. By restoring relationship at the heart of professional learning and development, we help to undo and protect against some of the stress and damage that competitive and individualistic academic culture normalizes. In this way, we also heal a potential divide between the relationally based practices we encourage with our teacher candidates and our own practices as scholars and colleagues, thus bringing more authenticity, depth, and integrity to our work as teacher educators.

Through self-study—and in particular our critical friendship—we have come to see that our intellectual and experiential understandings of mindful pedagogy and research cause us to challenge not just one another and our practice, but structures such as course design and lack of coherence between courses within our program. This is not to say that the work was not filled with tension. Members of our collaborative instructional team arrived with practices and assumptions grounded in years of experience, some of which clashed. Yet, as a group we negotiated our work within our university context while seeking to maintain social justice aims through situated and reflexive approaches to inquiry. Our critical friendship allowed us to open ourselves up to the struggle of working with colleagues who we felt shut down or dismissed by, and continue in our work rather than shrinking away.

We engaged with one another, our teacher candidates, and our colleagues in taking up the work of scholars such as Meyer, Greene, and Noddings, and exploring how their ideas relate to teaching, learning, and schooling. Through co-planning, co-teaching and co-reflecting, we constructed responsive, participatory, and social justice-oriented practices that effected change at the program structure level.

Through continuing to weave and construct possibilities together that enlarge the capacity of what each of us is able to do alone, we benefit from a co-regulated professional development practice that continues to emerge (Schnellert and Butler, 2014). Through critically mindful collaborative self study, we come to understand what is underneath what we say and do, revisit our intentions, and support, reposition or dismantle pedagogical and institutional practices and structures that divide us, put us in competition with one another, and seek to smooth out diversity and plurality.

REFERENCES

Berry, M. and Russell, T. (2014). Critical friends, collaborators and community in self-study. *Studying Teacher Education* 10, no. 3: 195–96.

Clandinin, D.J., Pushor, D., and Murray Orr, A. (2007). Navigating sites for narrative inquiry. *Journal of Teacher Education* 58, no. 1: 21–35

Etherington, K. (2007). Ethical research in reflexive relationships. *Qualitative Inquiry* 13, no. 7: 599–616.

Fels, L. and Belliveau, G. (2008). *Exploring curriculum: Performative inquiry, role drama and learning.* Vancouver, B.C.: Pacific Education Press.

Greene, M. (1978). *Learning landscapes.* New York: Teachers College Press.

Kreisberg, S. (1992). *Transforming power: Domination, empowerment and education.* Albany, NY: SUNY Press.

Malhotra-Bentz, V. and Shapiro, J. (1998). *Mindful inquiry in social research.* Thousand Oaks, CA: Sage.

Meyer, K. (2010). Living inquiry: Me, my self, and other. *Journal of Curriculum Theorizing* 26, no. 1: 85–96.

Moll, L. C. (2014). *L.S. Vygotsky and education.* New York: Routledge.

Noddings, N. (2002). *The challenge to care: An alternative approach to education.* New York: Teachers College Press.

Richardson, P. (2010). *Past buoy lines: An arts-based inquiry into living and knowing giftedness* (Unpublished doctoral dissertation). University of British Columbia, Vancouver.

Richardson, P. (2014). Dwelling artfully in the academy: Walking on precarious ground. In K. Ragoonaden (Ed.). *Contested sites in education: The quest for the public intellectual, identity and service.* New York: Peter Lang.

Richardson, P., Cherkowski, S., and Schnellert, L. (2015a). Awakeness, complexity and emergence: Learning through curriculum theory in teacher education. *Journal of the Canadian Association of Curriculum Studies* 13, no. 1: 138–67

Richardson, P., Schnellert, L., Broom, C., Cherkowski, S., and Lagrange, A. (May, 2015b). *Exploring an immersive, integrative, collaborative, inquiry-oriented approach to teacher education.* Paper presented at the Canadian Society for Studies in Education Conference. Ottawa, ON.

Routman, R. (2000). *Conversations.* Portsmouth, NH: Heinemann.

Samaras, A. P. (2011). *Self-study teacher research: Improving your practice through collaborative inquiry.* Thousand Oaks, CA: Sage.

Schnellert, L. and Butler, D.L. (2014). Collaborative inquiry: Empowering teachers in their professional development. *Education Canada* 54, no. 3: 18–22

Schnellert, L., Kozak, D., and Moore, S. (2015). Professional development that positions teachers as inquirers and possibilizers. *LEARNing Landscapes* 9, no. 1: 217–36.

Schnellert, L., Richardson, P., and Cherkowski, S. (2014). Teacher educator professional development as reflexive inquiry. *LEARNing Landscapes* 8, no. 1: 233–50.

Schnellert, L., Watson, L., and Widdess, N. (2015). *It's all about thinking: Building pathways for all learners in the middle years.* Winnipeg, MN: Portage and Main Press.

Stanley, S. (2012). Mindfulness: Towards a critical relational perspective. *Social and Personality Psychology Compass* 6: 631–41.

Varela, F. J., Thompson, E., and Rosch, E. (1991). *The embodied mind: Cognitive science and human experience.* Cambridge, MA: MIT.

FOUR

Critical Friends, Critical Insights

Developing a Dialogic Understanding of Practice-Based Teacher Education

Karen Rut Gísladóttir, Amy Johnson Lachuk, and Tricia DeGraff

> Relationships are at the heart of teaching. In practice-based teacher education the relationships have a particular quality to them that is different than relationships in a more theory-based teacher education. For instance, practice-based teacher education requires having close relationships. . . . If I want to teach a classroom at a school site I need to have buy-in from principals and at least one teacher eager to modify her classroom routine to accommodate my students. . . . The challenge of relationships ties into the challenge of time. —Amy Johnson Lachuk, personal narrative

These words are from a personal reflective narrative composed as part of a collaborative self-study (Pinnegar and Hamilton, 2010) of our practices as literacy teacher educators across three contexts—two urban universities in the Midwestern and Northeastern United States, respectively, and one at the University of Iceland. Amy encapsulates one of the key tensions within our work: managing the balance between time and relationships to develop a teacher education practice that better articulates the interplay between fieldwork and coursework. As collaborative inquirers, we examined how we engaged with such practice-based methods within our teacher education courses.

A practice-based approach to teacher education (PBTE) has a "systematic focus on developing teacher candidates' abilities to successfully enact high-leverage practices" (Zeichner, 2012 p. 378). Hollins (2011) explains a practice-based approach as "a mirror image of the practice of quality teaching in P–12 schools. This holistic practice-based approach integrates academic knowledge of theory, pedagogy, and curriculum across experiences in authentic contexts" (p. 395). The call for PBTE coursework has been amplified over the past two decades by policymakers' increased interest in the preparation of teachers (e.g., California State Bill 2042), which has emphasized meaningful connections between theory and practice, resulting in the use of practice-based methods. More recently, the adoption of the teacher performance assessment known as the edTPA (Stanford Center for Assessment, Learning, and Equity, 2013), in seven U.S. states has further mandated a change toward practice-based methods.

As teacher educators, we are enticed by practice-based methods and their promise of preparing prospective elementary teachers for the technical and practical demands of teaching. Yet, we also have felt tension between enacting practice-based methods and fulfilling our own commitments to ensuring that teacher candidates have the theoretical basis necessary for teaching for social justice (Zeichner, 2012). We believe that exploring our educational practices through self-study inquiry can increase our understandings of how we recruit our knowledge and experience to navigate this complex terrain in order to prepare teachers able to develop effective instructional practices while challenging the status quo.

While teacher education researchers point out the benefits and challenges of implementing PBTE, there are few reports of teacher educators actually living and experiencing such tension. Thus, we have inquired into our experiences with designing and implementing practice-based methods in our literacy instruction courses for preservice teacher candidates. We entered this self-study believing that by sharing and critically examining the accomplishments and challenges in our practice we will better understand our role in improving our program, teacher education, and educational reform movements (Samaras and Freese, 2006; Zeichner, 1999). In this chapter, we present a multivocal account (Guilfoyle et al., 1995; Pithouse-Morgan and Samaras, 2015; Schuck and Russell, 2005) of the processes we each went through in engaging with PBTE, and the role of critical friends in exploring these processes. The following questions guided this study:

- What can we learn about PBTE by collaborating as researchers and participants across international contexts in collaborative self-study?
- What can we learn about becoming literacy teacher educators and researchers across different contexts by participating as critical friends?

SELF-STUDY: THEORY AND METHODOLOGY

To address these questions, we engaged with a body of research on self-study within teacher education (Carter, 1993; Lyons and LaBoskey, 2002), in which self-study is understood as a form of reflection used to improve teacher education practice. This perspective goes beyond an understanding of practice as a set of predetermined skills and procedures of the "what, when, and how" to recognizing practice as shaped through interaction with personal, social, institutional, and cultural contexts (Clandinin, Huber, Steeves, and Li, 2011; Loughran, 2006; Pinnegar and Hamilton, 2010). Loughran (2006) suggests that in making such an understanding of teaching and learning visible, we lay a foundation for practices that allow us "to be responsive to the issues, needs and concerns of participants in ways that might make the unseen clear, the taken for granted questioned and the complex engaging" (p. 173). In developing a stance as self-study inquirers, we see our personal experiences in developing our practice-based methods as a source of new knowledge (Loughran and Northfield,1998) that we draw on to create new, authentic experiences and practices for ourselves and our students (Russell, 2002).

In self-study, relationships provide the foundation for understanding practice (Pinnegar and Hamilton, 2010; Samaras, 2011). In building a critical friendship triad in our collaborative self-study, we intended to create a space that would allow us to reflect upon personal experiences related to PBTE from multiple perspectives. Thus, our dialogue involved a process of coming-to-know within the context of this study and identifying opportunities for improving our practice (Pinnegar and Hamilton, 2010). Our collaboration was not meant to be evaluative, but provocative, giving us new perspectives from which to explore our assumptions and the complexity of our work (LaBoskey, 1997; Samaras, 2011, Pinnegar and Hamilton, 2010). The struggles and successes that emerged were not only nurtured through support and understanding, but also reinforced through opposition and resistance. In this sense, our dialogue both allowed us to come to terms with the teacher knowledge we were gaining as we engaged with practice-based methods (Loughran and Northfield, 1996) and revealed the ontological understandings and practical actions we developed through the process (Pinnegar and Hamilton, 2010). In keeping with the theme of this current collection, our collaborative inquiry enabled us to engage in our practices in a more mindful and open-hearted manner. Defined as a mind-body training that strengthens one's capacity to pay attention, nonjudgmentally, to one's thoughts, feelings, and body sensations, mindfulness nurtures the potential to develop a more skillful response to life's challenges (Soloway, Poulin, and Mackenzie, 2010). Within an educational context, Ek and Macintyre Latta (2013) posit that pedagogy is conceived as an ever-present process dwelling mindfully at the intersections of teaching/learning. As attention is turned to the space between teaching and learning, pedagogical significances are emphasized through mindful, open-hearted practices.

Context and Participants

Karen Rut Gísladóttir is a newer faculty member at a national university located in Iceland. As a new teacher educator, Karen is feeling pressure to engage her students with course material in a meaningful way. In entering this study she is beginning to see PBTE as a way to do so. Amy Johnson Lachuk is a literacy teacher educator at a college in a major metropolitan area in the United States. Recently, her state adopted a performance-based examination for initial teacher licensure, prompting significant changes to her practices. Tricia DeGraff taught for six years at an urban university in the Midwestern United States, where she played a critical role in reshaping the teacher education program using PBTE. Currently, she is a principal at an urban charter school, where she is using PBTE to help her teachers grow professionally. Having known each other professionally and personally for 12 years, our enduring relationship in the face of making desired changes to our practices prompted us to create a critical friendship where we could share, discuss, and challenge stories about our practices.

Data Generation and Analysis

Data generation for this self-study extended from January 2014 through September 2014. Data generation and analysis utilized narrative inquiry methods involving our "living stories" (Clandinin, 2013) as literacy teacher educators. We used inquiry to gain insight into our thoughts, beliefs and knowledge as we explored the benefits and challenges of implementing these practices, composed stories for each other, and re-lived our stories through written narrative and dialogue. We each wrote four stories about our use of a practice-based approach: 1) our arrival at this approach; 2) its benefits; 3) its challenges; 4) new opportunities for our practices and inquiry.

After exchanging written narratives, we read and responded to them using a double-entry journal format, recording points of interest in the first column and our responses or questions in the second. Following this analysis, we met via videoconference to discuss the journal entries, scrutinizing how we each responded to the narratives and identified narrative dimensions, but also corroborating, affirming, and interrogating each other's analyses. To structure our videoconferences, we used a modified version of the "save the last word for me" protocol (Averette, n.d.), in which each inquirer responded for two minutes to another's story, leaving the final two minutes for the author to respond. We listened to the audio recordings of these conversations during data analysis to inform the writing of the fifth narrative. Having gone through the process of analyzing our narratives, we concluded with writing a fifth story in which we reflected on our individual experiences of engaging in the process of this self-study, identifying how the dialogue was contributing to our understanding of becoming literacy teacher educators and researchers across different contexts.

A final step in our analysis was creating a reader's theater script to represent our conversations and narratives. We chose this format because we felt it best represented the complexity of bringing together and exploring our experiences (Donmoyer and Yennie-Donmoyer, 1995; Richardson and St. Pierre, 2008; Averette, n.d.) as critical friends. To construct our script, we followed a process similar to Donmoyer and Yennie-Donmoyer's (1995). We read through our analyses, identifying key elements from our narratives and audio-recorded conversations that supported our themes. We purposefully reconstructed these data to bring our voices and narratives into dialogue, using a script format. We identified five key themes related to our use of practice-based methods: a) negotiation of beliefs and practices, b) relationships and time, c) addressing diversity, d) institutional constraints, and e) alignment of practice-based methods. Below we present our findings as a reader's theater, in which we focus solely on three of these themes (due to space): relationships and time, diversity, and institutional constraints. We selected these because they seemed to have the most resonance for our practice. Like Adams and her colleagues (1998) found, bringing our three voices together into a reader's theater forefronts the "contradictions, tensions, and ambiguities that are embedded" (p. 384) in our practices as teacher educators.

READERS THEATER SCRIPT

What follows are interwoven segments from our discussions, contrasted against each other to reveal how we used dialogue to grapple with and elaborate on the complexity of our experiences.

Relationship and Time

Amy: In practice-based teacher education the relationships have a particular quality to them that is different than relationships in a more theory-based teacher education. . . . If I want to teach a classroom at a school-site I need to have buy-in from principals and at least one teacher eager to modify her classroom routine to accommodate my students.

Tricia: Yes, I don't think people who don't teach in this way realize how much of a time investment this is . . . building these relationships and working with practicing teachers and principals. It makes me better, but it takes time.

Amy: I agree. It seems like the biggest challenge is building relationships with schools and teachers that support this kind of work. That also takes time. However, it seems like we have to start somewhere. Will we ever really have enough time to have the greatest quality relationships with teachers/schools? . . . It seems like we are always in process in our relationships and even if we get them where we want them to be there is always room for growth and redefinition. I think we learn as much as we can to be as effective as we can be at that moment in time.

Tricia: I like the way you think about it. In determining the best way to work in the field site, I think it is ideal to have time to talk with the teachers in the building, but I struggle to find the time to meet with them. They have so little time to use for their own planning and preparation that they don't necessarily want to spend a lot of time planning with me. So I know that there are missed opportunities for collaboration with teachers in the field site.

Amy: I see the challenge of relationships tying into the challenge of time. Simply put, crafting and cultivating relationships with teachers and principals requires time. This is not something that one can "jump into." At USC, I remember how when I taught courses on-site my first semester, it was at a school with which we already had a strong relationship. When I decided to change to a more culturally and socioeconomically diverse school, I did so through a literacy coach whom I knew and who taught as an adjunct at the university. So, starting to teach a course on site at a local elementary school is difficult when one is a new faculty member. At Hunter College, one of my secret hopes is that a former student will step up and welcome me into her classroom.

Tricia: This would certainly ease the transition . . . there is a comfort working with people we have taught. In response to learning that graduates from our program did not feel prepared to teach writing, I decided to model the teaching of writing in the field site. I worked with a former of student and first-year teacher to plan and teach a four-week writing unit, going through the writing process from pre-writing to publication. I explained that I would like to bring my students into the classroom twice a week to observe the writing unit. He was excited to participate. This was safe for me, because I had a good relationship with this former student and as his former instructor, I felt comfortable entering his classroom.

Amy: I LOVE THIS!

Tricia: Throughout this experience, I systematically collected reflections and other written data pieces and analyzed data. I learned a lot from this experience, including that research makes me a better instructor. And this collaboration led to working with other teachers. Last year I modeled the writing unit in a first grade teacher's classroom who I never dreamed of being able to share classroom space with. This helped me see that building these relationships that allow us to have access to classrooms takes time. I started teaching the writing unit with a former student, but over time was able to forge relationships with other teachers.

Amy: Building relationships takes time, but I see time as a factor in another sense. Designing course assignments that connect to the field requires time, yes, but also flexibility. For example, I am designing an assignment for a teacher candidate to carry out through an unknown context. . . . When I ask students, for instance, to observe a read aloud or collect reading logs, I assume that these are practices that their cooperating teachers engage in. I have learned this is not always the case. I grapple with how ethical it is to tie students' grades to contexts that are out of their control.

Tricia: This is such a challenge. . . . In the writing unit I discussed, the preservice teachers engaged in focused inquiry and directed observation, but they did not have the opportunity to engage in guided practice. And, many of them did not have the opportunity to teach writing in this way during student teaching. Thus, I'm not quite sure how much they actually learned from this experience . . . I know they learned about the developmental process of teaching writing, learned more about the importance of student voice and choice, and they were able to articulate ideas about how they think they would teach writing, but I'm not sure what they could actually enact. This is one of the things I need to think about as I transition to the role of principal.

Addressing (Academic, Cultural and Linguistic) Diversity

Tricia: When I began teaching my course in the field site, it was messy. In trying to refine my courses each year, there are parts that still feel 'messy.' I don't mind being thrown into a situation and making my way through the messiness. But, I am coming to an understanding that I operate from a different stance from my students; thus I don't always understand their discomfort. Some of them really want to be given exact steps to follow in order to become a good teacher. I teach them that they have to jump in and start trying things, before they know everything . . . because you learn more if you attempt something and begin to understand the complexity of what you are trying . . . and that is messy. I also know that good teachers constantly adapt and don't follow a recipe. In working to enact constructivism as a teacher educator, interns experience discomfort at times.

Amy: I have this same challenge. I try to be explicit with the connections between course readings and practice, yet they still don't have a firm grasp on the concepts presented in course readings . . . I feel like they don't feel like they've experienced the readings unless they are dissecting them.

Tricia: In spite of these challenges there are numerous advantages to PBTE. One is that I feel my interns operate with a sense of urgency. They see the relevance of course readings, experiences, assignments more than when I taught at the university.

Amy: I am struggling because I do not see my students engaging with course texts. If they create instructional materials, they usually come from the Internet and are not reflective of what they are encountering in their texts. Just yesterday, a student sent me a packet of reading response worksheets that she had basically copied off the Internet. She thinks responding to the text using each one of these worksheets will help students really "engage" in their independent reading. I had to hold back expressing my disappointment at this choice. I know she sent them to me for my approval, but I simply encouraged her to use the Reading Log form I had provided in class. I just don't want them to think that teaching requires "fancy" worksheets.

Tricia: I remember that when I taught at the university students would complain that the readings were repetitive, or say things about their observations that showed judgment of teachers and really dismissed the complexity of teaching. I remember feeling frustrated that they didn't understand just how hard teaching is. In a practice-based course, they experience the complexity. They know what it feels like for a lesson to flop; to ask a question of a student and not get a response. One of my former students said that this experience allowed him to experience the 'curveballs' of teaching. I also feel they get to practice discussing difficult issues with students and confronting their own identity and biases. One of my former students—white, male—began the year talking about the surrounding community in demeaning terms, and said that we shouldn't talk about complex issues with kids—that was the counselor's job. Later in the semester, he read *Ron's Big Mission* to his group of students that included African American boys. As he read the book and Ron was denied the privilege of borrowing books from the public library, the students started talking about the racist people in the book. My student came back to class, asking how he could talk about race. He said he wanted to address their comments, but he didn't want to sound like he was defending white people . . . he wanted to know more about how he could talk about race with students. His experiences with children changed him.

Karen: It sounds like working within authentic contexts makes this experience meaningful to students. I can relate to that. Through my teacher inquiry I remember struggling with making connections between my practice and the sociocultural theories of language and literacy learning and teaching I was reading at the time. At first it was as if I was working on two fronts. On the one hand, I was recording my teaching experiences in the teaching journal. On the other hand, I found myself nodding my head at the ideas in the literature I was reading—they made so much sense! The real challenge began when I tried to connect the theories to my observations, and the concepts I read about began to take on new forms. My great challenge was to understand what these ideas meant and how they emerged within the context of the classroom. Reading through my journal, I note that the first step in connecting the two territories was to begin creating questions from the theories in relation to what I was experiencing in the classroom. Slowly, my journal entries changed from questions like "Why can't my students just complete the assignments instead of complaining about them?" to questions like "What is keeping my students' strengths hidden?"

Amy: I love this question. I need to start asking this more. Instead of "Why aren't my students doing X?" I need to think "Why aren't I able to see what my students are capable of doing? What tools would better assist me?" I want to share this with my students. I think it is profound. One of my underlying concerns, though, is how well we support teacher candidates in teaching diverse learners. In terms of multicultural education, I believe it is not about teaching cultures explicitly, but about planning instructional experiences that engage with learners academically, culturally and linguistically.

Tricia: Interns have become angry at me for challenging them for saying something insensitive. Just the other day, a graduating student told me that he "hated" (his word) me for an incident that happened early in his internship, but now he knows that he learned a lot from this experience. Another graduating student, also recently referenced that event as a key learning experience in an informal conversation with me. The event referenced by both students is an event that I wrote reflections about because it caused a difficult few weeks for the interns and me. The event basically consisted of a student saying something about the "sketchy" neighborhoods where our classes are held. When I heard this comment in class, I challenged the interns to think about what that comment meant and this ended up being a difficult, 30-minute conversation that could have lasted longer. It was a conversation that made many interns, mostly the white interns, mad at me. Many of the black students appreciated that I didn't let the comment go unnoticed, because they felt that "sketchy" was being used to describe their childhood communities. I believe this based on their reflections, things students told me later, the dynamic of the class after that event, and what they have told me since then. It was uncomfortable to be in the position of making people angry. And, I know that often, we have to make people "angry" or at least uncomfortable for their own learning. This means there are moments when I have to confront people and ask difficult questions.

Amy: We as teacher educators sometimes get seduced by the idea that education and learning must always be comfortable, that every answer is correct, and that we don't want to push students too hard in fear that they will "hate" us, and thus not learn from us. As I get older and (arguably) wiser, I think learning often requires some discomfort. To grow and learn we have to learn to experience discomfort and grow through it. Not everything will come easily and it is that struggle that allows us to endure and persist. It is through struggling with discomfort that we develop confidence in our abilities and intellect. I once told students, "I know this is making you uncomfortable, and I'm okay with that." Boy, did I get some glares. But in the end, it worked out because they persisted through the discomfort and learned. That being said, I was supportive of them in grappling with their discomfort. When they would complain, I'd say: "What did you learn? You are doing great. Keep taking small steps. Just be 'uncomfortable' enough so that you are able to learn. If you think you're not learning, then pull back into your comfort zone, until you are ready to feel a bit more discomfort."

Tricia: I also think about the complexity of multicultural education and teaching for social justice . . . it is hard to make sense of all of this. . . . Asking our pre-service teachers to read articles won't necessarily help them "get it," but some articles might support them in understanding . . . and it can't happen in one course alone.

Karen: When I listen to you I think about the underlying reason for the tension I am experiencing as I transition into academia. I'm realizing that it is important to me to continue developing the teacher identity I began developing when teaching children who are deaf. I spent nine years making sense of the reality of the classroom I was working within, and in trying to understand what kind of teacher I wanted to become. It was important for me as a teacher to create learning spaces within the classroom for students to bring to bear the language and cultural resources they brought to school. I'm revisiting these classroom experiences—exploring the "messiness"—in trying to make sense of the multiple threads influencing that reality. Many times, I didn't know where I was going; I only heard the echoes of my questions regarding my practice, my ruminations about the intention of my work, and my doubts that I was moving in the right direction. This taught me that it takes more than telling teachers what they need to do in order to develop learning contexts that build on the diverse backgrounds of students. It takes time, critical reflection, collaboration, and vulnerability to recognize and change the references that influence the way we teach and rationalize our practice.

Amy: I am curious how you share these insights with pre-service teacher candidates. I want to hear more about how a "resource" or "asset" model informs your teacher education practice. What practices do you use to help teacher candidates inquire into the assets that children bring with them into the classroom?

Karen: This is probably a part of the tension I am experiencing. I feel strongly about the importance of student teachers engaging in inquiry, but I wonder how to facilitate their work of engaging critically with their practices, identifying and altering deficit assumptions about students. It is a vulnerable process that requires trust.

Institutional Constraints

Amy: I have also learned that institutional constraints play a huge role in implementing PBTE. One constraint I face is that at Hunter we try to meet the needs of many different kinds of students. We have 2 slots for evening classes, 4:30–7:00 and then 7:00–9:30. Students often take back-to-back classes in the evening. It would be difficult for a student to get from a school site back to Hunter to take another evening class. Likewise, it would be difficult in NYC to host an on-site class in the evening, as the school buildings are closed.

Tricia: Yes, this is a real challenge. We used to have an evening track and a daytime track. When we reformed our program to make it entirely field-based, we eliminated our evening track after much discussion.

Amy: So many complications. I had the idea of starting an after-school literacy club at one school, where my Hunter students would work with a group of struggling readers. These students would be handpicked by the principal, but I was told this would not be possible at a New York City public school. So, now I am having to think more creatively about how to make this happen.

Tricia: Yes, you have many GREAT ideas . . . aren't the institutional constraints frustrating! When we discuss them in my context, I often think they seem silly. We actually have been able to work through quite a few of them, but you have to work collaboratively. If you are the only person in support of this work, some might use institutional constraints to block you!

Karen: These institutional constraints were also present when I entered an elementary school site in Iceland as a doctoral student conducting teacher inquiry for my PhD. I hoped my colleagues would consider initiating their own research projects. But just raising the topic worked to silence my colleagues. Several times, I heard someone say "research?" in a tone that indicated they were thinking about the idea, but then this was followed by an attitude that conveyed, "I don't have the time to do it. My responsibility is to teach."

Tricia: While I was teaching in the classroom, I always wanted to find time to research my practice, but never could. Now that I see how much researching my practice helps me improve, I think we MUST find the time as practitioners . . . how can we carve out that time? I want to keep this at the forefront of my mind as I set out to lead my school. Please help hold me accountable.

IMPLICATIONS OF OUR WORK

As teaching is a complex, dynamic arrangement of many factors, reflecting on and changing practice is not always easy. However, the other side of complexity is simplicity (Palmer, 1998)—for complexity is undergirded by some simple actions and solutions. For instance, the complexity of teaching diverse learners is foregrounded by the simple actions of treating every human being with dignity. Amy captured this well in a question she posed in her last narrative where we discussed what we had learned about education through engaging in this study: "If we know that teaching is complex, then it really isn't that complex, is it?" Underlying the complexity of teaching are some really simple behaviors—listening closely and looking carefully at children's learning processes; being present and mindful in the moment, so one can make decisions that respond to children's humanity, uplifting them; making decisions based on what one sees and hears, and what one knows about children's literacy development. These complex ideas are constituted of simple parts. Through self-study we engaged in reflective inquiry (Korthagen, 2013), which led to deeper insights into our teaching practices and brought a greater sense of mindfulness to our teaching. A dialogic process of constructing, sharing, and interpreting our teaching stories allowed us to reflect on our practice and articulate our interpretations of this practice. This type of critical friendship provided us with a community of reflective colleagues supporting an organic and emergent professional development conceived as an ever-present process dwelling mindfully at the intersections of teaching and learning.

REFERENCES

Adams, N., Causey, T., Jacobs, M. E. Munro, P., and Trousdale, A. (1998). Womentalkin': A reader's theater performance of teachers' stories. *International journal of qualitative studies in education* 11, no. 3: 383–95

Averette, P. (n.d.). *Save the last word for ME.* Retrieved from http://www.nsrfharmony.org/system/files/protocols/save_last_word_0.pdf.

Carter, K. (1993). The place of story in the study of teaching and teacher education. *Educational Researcher* 22, no. 1: 5–12.

Clandinin, D. J. (2013). *Engaging in narrative work.* Walnut Creek, CA: Left Coast Press.

Clandinin, D.J., Huber, J., Steeves, P., and Li, Y. (2011). Becoming a narrative inquirer: Learning to attend within the three-dimensional narrative inquiry space. In S. Trahar (Ed.), *Learning and teaching narrative inquiry: Travelling in the borderlands* (pp. 33–51). The Netherlands: John Benjamins.

Donmoyer, R., and Yennie-Donmoyer, J. (1995). Data as drama: Reflections on the use of readers theater as a mode of qualitative data display. *Qualitative Inquiry* 1: 402–28.

Ek, A. and Macintyre Latta, M. (2013). Preparing to teach: Redeeming the potentialities of the present through conversations of practice, education and culture. *The Journal of the John Dewey Society* 29, no. 1: 84–104.

Guilfoyle, K., Hamilton. M. L., Pinnegar, S., and Placier, M. (1995). Becoming teachers of teachers: The paths of four beginners. In T. Russell and F. Korthagen (Eds.), *Teachers who teach teachers: Reflection on teacher education.* London: Falmer Press.

Hollins, E.R. (2011). Teacher preparation for quality teaching. *Journal of teacher education* 62, no. 4: 395–407.

Karthagen, F. (2013). The care reflection approach. In F. Karthagen, Y. Kim, and W. Egreen (Eds.), *Teaching and learning from within: A care reflection approach to quality and inspriation in education.* New York: Routledge.

LaBoskey, V. K. (1997). Teaching to teach with purpose and passion: Pedagogy for reflective practice. In J. Loughran and T. Russell (Eds.), *Teaching about teaching: Purpose, passion and pedagogy in teacher education.* London: Falmer Press.

Loughran, J. (2006). *Developing a pedagogy of teacher education: Understanding teaching and learning about teaching.* New York: Routledge.

Loughran, J. and Northfield, J. (1998). A framework for the development of self-study practice. In M. L. Hamilton, S. Pinnegar, T. Russell, and V. K. LaBosky (Eds.), *Reconceptualizing teaching practice: Self-study in teacher education* (pp. 7–18). London: Falmer Press.

Lyons, B., and LaBosky, V. K. (2002). *Narrative inquiry in practice: Advancing the knowledge of teaching.* New York: Teachers College Press.

Palmer, P.J. (1998). *The courage to teach: exploring the inner landscape of a teacher's life.* San Franciso, CA: Jossey-Bass.

Pinnegar, S. and Hamilton, M. L. (2010). *Self-Study of practice as a genre of qualitative research.* The Netherlands: Springer.

Pithouse-Morgan, K., and Samaras, A. P. (2015). The power of "we" for professional learning. In K. Pithouse-Morgan and A. P. Samaras (Eds.), *Polyvocal professional learning through self-study research.* The Netherlands: Sense Publisher.

Richardson, L. and St. Pierre, E. A. (2005). Writing: A method of inquiry. In N. K. Denzin and Y. S. Lincoln (Eds.), *Collecting and interpreting qualitative materials* (pp. 473–99). Thousand Oaks, CA: Sage.

Russell, T. (2002). Can self-study improve teacher education? In J. Loughran and T. Russell (Eds.), *Improving teacher education practices through self-study* (pp. 3–9). New York: Routledge/Falmer.

Samaras, A. P. (2011). *Self-study teacher research: Improving your practice through collaborative inquiry*. Thousand Oaks, CA: Sage.

Samaras, A. P. and Freese, A. (2006). *Self-study of teaching practices*. New York: Peter Lang.

Schuck, S., and Russell, T. (2005). Self-study, critical friends and the complexities of teacher education. *Studying teacher education: A journal of self-study of teacher education practice* 1, no. 2: 107–21.

Soloway, G., Poulin. P., and Mackenzie, C. S. (2010). Preparing new teachers for the full catastrophe of the 21st century classroom: Integrating mindfulness into initial teacher education. In A. Cohan and A. Honingsfeld (Eds.) *Breaking the mold of pre-service and in-service teacher education: Innovative and successful pratices for the 21st century*. Lanham, MD: Rowman and Littlefield Education.

Stanford Center for Assessment, Learning, and Equity (2013). *edTPA elementary education: Assessment handbook*.

Zeichner, K. (1999). The new scholarship in teacher education. *Educational Researcher* 28, no. 9: 4–15.

Zeichner, K. (2012). The turn once again toward practice-based teacher education. *Journal of teacher education* 63, no. 5: 376–82.

FIVE

Critical Friendship, Mindfulness, and the Philosophy for Children Hawai'i Approach to Teaching and Learning

Amber Strong Makaiau, Jessica Ching-Sze Wang,
Karen Ragoonaden, Lu Leng, and
Heather M. DeWoody

This chapter investigates the relationship between philosophy for children Hawai'i (p4cHI), critical friendship, and mindfulness. It is situated within the context of an international online collaborative journaling project that began in 2014 (Makaiau, Leng, and Fukui, 2015), and that continues to be carried out by four of the authors of this chapter. Brought together because of our shared interests in p4cHI (Jackson, 2001; Makaiau and Miller, 2012) and self-study research methodologies (Loughran, 2007; Beck, Freese, and Kosnik, 2004; Samaras and Freese, 2006), we are teacher educators and p4cHI practitioners from the USA, Taiwan, Canada, and China. In 2015 we engaged in an international online collaborative journaling project to:

- Expand the culturally responsive international p4cHI research collective that was initially created by Makaiau, Leng, and Fukui (2015)
- Explore the role of a p4cHI teacher/facilitator with international partners
- Reflect on the professional and personal impact of belonging to an international research collective

- Disseminate and mobilize knowledge relating to the professional development of teacher educators, practitioners, and researchers involved in the worldwide Philosophy for Children movement

As a result of the findings that emerged (Makaiau, Wang, Ragoonaden, and Leng, In Press), and at the suggestion of Karen Ragoonaden (also an editor of this book) we developed an interest in exploring how the p4cHI approach to teaching and learning promoted critical friendship and mindfulness in our international online collaborative journaling project.

In this chapter we report on the most recent analysis that we conducted to examine how the "four pillars" of p4cHI (community, inquiry, philosophy, and reflection) (Jackson, 2013, p. 99–109) contributed to the development of critical friendship and mindfulness in the professional work that we accomplished while journaling with one another from August 2014 to January 2015. We share how we used the methods of constant comparison (Glaser and Strauss, 1967) and the four pillars of p4cHI to re-examine close to eighty pages of journal entries and written dialogue that are housed in an online Google document. In our findings we use quotes from our online journal to illustrate how the four pillars of p4cHI provided us with both the theoretical framework and the practical tools for building an "intellectually safe" community (Jackson, 2001, p. 460) and for conducting "systematic and critical examination of [our] actions and [our] context as a path to develop a more consciously driven mode of professional activity" (Samaras and Freese, 2006, p. 11). At the chapter's conclusion we expound on how the four pillars of p4cHI enabled us to co-construct a community of critical friendship and to engage in a collectively mindful process that deepened the understanding of self, other, and our professional practice.

Background and Theoretical Framework

In this section we provide the background and theoretical context for the chapter by reviewing the literature related to philosophy for children Hawai'i (p4cHI), Self-Study of Teacher Education Practices (S-STEP), critical friendship, and mindfulness.

PHILOSOPHY FOR CHILDREN HAWAI'I (P4cHI)

Philosophy for children Hawai'i (p4cHI) is Thomas Jackson's (2001, 2012) teacher-lead and culturally responsive offshoot of Matthew Lipman's original worldwide Philosophy for Children movement. It is an innovative approach to education that transforms the schooling experience by engaging learners in the activity of philosophy. P4cHI practitioners convert traditional classrooms into "intellectually safe" (Jackson, 2001, p. 460) communities of inquiry where students and teachers co-create and co-construct their abilities to think for themselves in responsible ways. Defined by both a theoretical framework and actual set of classroom strategies, p4cHI is best characterized as a philosopher's pedagogy (Makaiau and Miller, 2012) that can be adapted and molded to fit the needs of students in a wide range of educational settings and cultural contexts.

The theoretical framework that supports the p4cHI approach to teaching and learning is referred to in the literature as the four pillars of p4cHI (Jackson, 2013; Makaiau and Miller, 2012). These four pillars are: community, inquiry, philosophy, and reflection. Designed to support p4cHI practitioners as they find their way and construct a p4cHI practice of their very own, the four pillars of p4cHI are the conceptual blueprints from which all p4cHI activities and assessments are built upon. Some of the most common p4cHI activities include co-constructing an intellectually safe classroom, creating a "community ball" (Jackson, 2001, p. 461; Makaiau, 2015, p. 2–3) to mediate turn taking, using the "Good Thinker's Tool Kit" to ask questions and make claims (Jackson, 2001, p. 463), engaging in "Plain Vanilla" inquiry procedure (p. 462), and using evaluation criteria to reflect on progress made by the community of inquiry (Makaiau, 2015, p. 3). In the section that follows, we give a brief description of each pillar, and later on the chapter we provide excerpts from our journal to explain how the four pillars helped to cultivate and nurture critical friendship and mindfulness in our professional practice.

Community

Central to the philosophy for children Hawai'i approach is the idea that teaching and learning must be done in an "intellectually safe" community of inquiry. Participants work together to create conditions where students and teachers feel emotionally and intellectually secure and free to "ask virtually any question or state any view so long as respect for all is honored" (Jackson, 2013, p. 460). The community practices "listening, thoughtfulness, silence, care and respect for the thoughts of others" (Jackson, 2001, p. 459). To establish and maintain this type of community, p4cHI practitioners recognize that intellectually safe communities of inquiry do not always form naturally; instead, they must be cultivated and nurtured by both students and teachers (Makaiau, 2015). This includes ensuring that there is ongoing process in which the group can co-construct, co-create, and reflect on the definitions of intellectual safety and community. What develops out of this sense of community is a growing trust among the participants and the ensuing courage to present one's own thoughts.

Inquiry

In p4cHI, inquiry is learner-centered, which means that it "arises out of the questions and interests of the community" (Jackson, 2001, p. 462). It is facilitated with instructional strategies like "Plain Vanilla" and "The Good Thinker's Tool Kit" (Jackson, 2012, p. 103–6), which help participants engage in democratic praxis (Makaiau, 2015) and "dig beneath the surface" (Lukey, 2013, p. 50) of the topics that they are inquiring about. The permeating spirit of the inquiry *is not being in a rush* (Jackson, 2001); it emphasizes instead an "ongoing inquiry to modify, correct, enhance and deepen our views of the world" and ourselves (Makaiau and Miller, 2012, p. 10). Progress in an inquiry is characterized and evaluated using the following questions: What new ideas emerged? Were new connections made? Did you get more confused or see the complexity of the topic? Did a possible answer develop? What new questions do you have?

Philosophy

Practitioners of the philosophy for children Hawai'i approach to teaching and learning like to distinguish between *Big P* and *little p* philosophy (Jackson, 2012). In *little p* philosophy the emphasis is on the activity of philosophy, on doing. Like all philosophy it begins in wonder—our own deep wonder about ourselves and about the world around us. p4cHI practitioners refine their wonderings with cognitive tools, which help them to think/question more deeply about their own experiences and subjects such as science, math, and history. In *little p* philosophy, content is reconceptualized as "the interaction between the participants' beliefs and experiences and subject matter they are inquiring about" (Makaiau and Miller, 2012, p. 10). It is "the set of beliefs that we all possess to make sense of the world and hence is unique to each of us . . . it is the result of the particularities of what some philosophers refer to as our 'situatedness' in the world and our responses to them" (Jackson, 2012, p. 5). "This shift in perspective moves philosophy from canonical texts and the problems of philosophy to the activity of inquiry" (Makaiau and Miller, 2012, p. 10). When we engage in the type of philosophical inquiry that is characterized by *little p* philosophy, we are engaging in on-going philosophical reflection. We are living what Socrates referred to as the "examined life" (Plato, 1938/1961, p. 38a).

Reflection

Finally, the p4cHI approach provides participants with instruments for engaging in an iterative process of self-reflection and self-correction (Makaiau, 2015). P4cHI practitioners and participants use reflective questions, dialogue, inquiry, and cognitive tools to think through the "trying" and "undergoing" of personal and collective life experiences (Dewey, 1916, p. 146). They thoughtfully respond to diverse perspectives/points of view and explore possible meanings and connections to deepen the inquiry, enhance self-knowledge, and understanding of the world around them. They think about their own thinking, actions and emotions, and they examine the relationship between self, other, and their environment (Makaiau, 2010). In their reflections, p4cHI practitioners and participants are encouraged to generate conclusions about how meaningful and connected specific knowledge is to self-understanding and understanding of the world (Makaiau, 2014).

Bound together by these four pillars, philosophy for children Hawai'i practitioners are now found in a number of locations across the globe, and researchers like us, who are working to study p4cHI in a wide range of geo-sociopolitical contexts, need methods that bend to the interests of our diverse backgrounds and facilitate a common ground for us to discuss and to reflect together. It is for these reasons that we turned to S-STEP, which is a research methodology used by teachers and teacher educators to create structures for ongoing professional development (Beck, Freese, and Kosnik, 2004; Macintyre and Buck, 2007) in a variety of cultural contexts.

SELF-STUDY OF TEACHER EDUCATION PRACTICES (S-STEP)

Growing rapidly in breadth and depth in the last twenty years, S-STEP situates teaching and learning at the nexus of educational research. It is one of the largest Special Interest Groups (SIG) in the American Educational Research Association (AERA) and publishes its own journal *Studying Teacher Education.* Aware that the literature points to a plethora of models related to the professional development of teacher educators, we posit that S-STEP, by virtue of its focus on a systematic "personal-constructivist-collaborative" (Beck, Freese, and Kosnik, 2004, p. 1256) approach to critical self-reflection, provides a culturally-responsive (Makaiau and Freese, 2013) and organic paradigm for promoting and sustaining excellence in practice. We have found this to be especially true when it is conducted with international partners (Makaiau, Leng, and Fukui, 2015) who are open to "constructing . . . learning together, probing one another's ideas, and reviewing and reframing . . . ideas collaboratively" (Kosnik, Samaras, and Freese, 2006, p. 153). In relationship to the questions being explored in this chapter, critical friendship and mindfulness are two interconnected and highly desired practices of international S-STEP teacher researchers, like us, who aim to collectively engage in methods that are both personally and professionally meaningful.

Critical Friendship

One of the most important considerations in the methodology of self-study is the concept of critical friendship. Illustrated by the findings from previous research studies, the critical friend method supports the identification and strengthening of shared values concerning practice; improves teaching through critical and collaborative self-reflection; facilitates communication between colleagues; and it helps to foster a professional community of inquiry that is characterized by innovation and creation (Costa and Kallick, 1993; Samaras, 2011; Schuck and Russell, 2005). When self-study researchers collaborate with critical friends they gain immediate access to a colleague's expertise and feedback, which enables continued professional development.

Ragoonaden and Bullock (2016) acknowledge that critical friendships must be nurtured in a climate of trust, compassion, and empathy. They posit that it must encourage analysis and integrity, and it should culminate with an advocacy for success. In addition, they explain that critical friendship requires a connection on a socio-emotional level as well as a formal process based on criticality. To support their claims, Hultman Özek, Edgren, and Jandér (2012) provide a succinct review of the many emergent definitions of critical friendship in contemporary professional literature. They explain that the necessary conditions for successful critical friendship are trust, constructive criticality a critically, professionalism, and knowledge of a critical friends teaching context and environment. Further, Hultman Özek et al's. (2012) literature review advances that the critical friend should be implemented as professional development in a collaborative setting rather than a formal hierarchical method for peer observation (Baskerville and Goldblatt, 2009; Biggs and Tang, 2007; Swaffield, 2007).

Mindfulness

Mindfulness Training (MT) is a reflective mind-body practice that is recognized as a means to support the various facets of well-being in a variety of contexts. Secular in nature, mindful based training allows the individual to develop the ability to focus through breathing exercises, which promote increased awareness and attention. Given the success of mindfulness interventions with a range of populations, it is logical to explore how a reflective mind-body practice relates to S-STEP, critical friendship, and philosophy for children Hawai'i.

Described as "the awareness that emerges through paying attention on purpose, in the present moment, and non-judgmentally to the unfolding of experience moment by moment" (Kabat-Zinn, 2003, p. 145), the reflective body-mind practice of mindfulness can support the often stressful and challenging contexts of teaching and learning. Since mindfulness' focus on attention and awareness is considered to be an innate and inherent human quality, this practice can be integrated into the lived and examined experiences of a teacher educator's practice (Plato, 1938/ 1961; Ragoonaden, 2015). Further, a mindful and reflective practice (Sheets, 2005; Samaras, Hicks, and Garvey, 2004) in educational contexts can sustain Schön's (1983) concept of *reflection in action* by not being in a rush, by paying attention, being present, and being aware of one's every day activities, particularly when those activities center on a situation in which the outcome is uncertain.

In terms of the professional development of teachers, Poulin et al. (2008) and Meiklejohn et al. (2012) state:

> Early research results on three illustrative mindfulness-based teacher training initiatives suggest that personal training in mindfulness skills can increase teachers' sense of well-being and teaching self-efficacy, as well as their ability to manage classroom behavior and establish and maintain supportive relationships with students. (p. 291)

In addition, MT has been shown to cultivate innovations in pedagogy by enhancing learning, health, well-being, and positive human development (Mackenzie, 2015).

Interested in building on this emergent field of MT research in the context of education we explored already established connections between mindfulness and the professional development of Philosophy for Children practitioners. This led us to the work of Will Ord. As a former chair of the Society for the Advancement of Philosophical Enquiry and Reflection in Education, Ord is a seasoned Philosophy for Children practitioner who also writes and teaches about MT. He explains,

> Mindfulness is about training the mind to be a "wonderful servant rather than a terrible master" (old Taoist saying). Isn't it strange that we learn about hundreds of topics at school, but never about the actual thing that does all the learning/experiencing/feeling/thinking itself— the mind! Mindfulness helps to redress this extraordinary omission in education (Ord, 2016).

To extend Ord's work and to become more aware of the number of complex components that contributed to the success of our international online collaborative journaling project, we made the decision to re-analyze the journal that we kept in 2015 so that we could examine how the four pillars of p4cHI, self-study methodologies, and online journaling with international partners provided us with a space to learn and grow as critical friends and mindful scholar practitioners.

RESEARCH QUESTIONS

The following research questions were used to guide this study: What does our collaborative online journal teach us about the relationship between mindfulness, critical friendship, and philosophy for children Hawai'i (p4cHI)? What do we mean by critical friendship? Mindfulness? How does the p4cHI approach to teaching and learning promote critical friendship and mindfulness in an international online collaborative journaling project created by four teacher educators from the USA, Taiwan, Canada, and China?

DATA SOURCES

Data came from the interactive online journal that Amber Makaiau, Jessica Wang, Karen Ragoonaden, and Lu Leng kept with two other colleagues, Mitsuyo Toyoda from Japan and Ann Yeh from Tawain who eventually dropped out of the project due to a number of professional and personal reasons. We wrote in the journal at least once a week, for six months (8/28/2014–1/8/2015) and used Google documents to share our writing with one another in a "live" online setting. Following Elliott-Johns, Peterson, Allison-Roan, and Ramirez's (2010) work, our journals "included personal reflections, perceptions and questions" (p. 81). At the end of our data collection period, we had 78 pages of single-spaced journal entries and written dialogue. Secondary data sources included emails and analytic memos (Charmaz, 2006; Creswell, 2007).

DATA ANALYSIS

The initial analysis of the data occurred in 2015 and the methods used are fully described in a chapter authored by Makaiau, Wang, Ragoonaden, and Leng (In Press). Then, for this additional research project we used the methods of constant comparison (Glaser and Strauss, 1967) and the four pillars of p4cHI to re-examine the journal entries and written dialogue that were stored in our online Google document. This occurred in three phases.

In phase one, we worked individually to develop initial open codes and analytic themes (Charmaz, 2006). Then, we came together via email and used dialogue methodology (Lunenberg and Samaras, 2011) to share our open codes and reflect on the challenges we each faced as we revisited the massive amount of data that we had collected during our original study. Characteristic of critical friends (Miles and Huberman, 1994), we asked questions of one another, explored possible answers to our questions, gained new perspectives, and further examined the quotes we were using to develop our open codes. Through this rich exchange of ideas we made a connection between the data we were analyzing, the four pillars of p4cHI, critical friendship, and mindfulness. This led us into phase two of the data analysis process, which included coming to a consensus on the definition of the four pillars of p4cHI. Then, we worked individually again to use the definitions we developed to find quotes related to community, inquiry, philosophy, and reflection. Finally, we came back together again, shared quotes, and moved into the process of axial coding (Strauss and Corbin, 1998) to "specif[y] the properties and dimensions of a category," and relate "categories to subcategories" (Charmaz, 2006, p. 60). This helped us bring our data back "together again in a coherent whole" (Charmaz, 2006, p. 60). In phase three, we wrote up our findings and collaborated further to revise and refine our thinking.

FINDINGS

The findings that emerged from this most recent analysis of the data are organized around the four pillars of philosophy for children Hawai'i: community, inquiry, philosophy, and reflection. In the ensuing discussions, parallels to the larger themes of mindfulness and critical friendship are established to demonstrate their impact on our professional development.

Pillar One: Community

At the very beginning of our journaling project we worked with one another to establish and build an intellectually safe community of inquiry. This started with Amber establishing a list of eight journaling guidelines. Number five on this list stated, "create and maintain an "intellectually safe" (Jackson, 2001) journaling environment with the other participants in this project" (8/28/15). As a part of this process, Amber also invited everyone to write down "three things you want others to know about you" (8/28/14). From this sharing, we got to know about our colleagues' purpose for participating in the international self-study journals as well as some background information about families, interests, values, and educational practices.

Who Are We as a Community?

The first of these introductory journal entries came from Lulu, and then followed by Jessica, Amber, and Karen.

> Because my internship teaching experiences with kindergarteners in Qingdao City in China made me realize how I wanted to be a teacher. As an educator I feel I can always grow personally and professionally; I

need to learn from others and from myself throughout my lifetime. (Lulu, 8/28/14)

I am a professor in teacher education and I am also a religious practitioner. I love my professional work. And I am also deeply involved in my religion to promote the notion of self-cultivation. My religion combines Confucianism, Buddhism, and Daoism, with the goal of helping people uplift their lives and realize a more humane world. (Jessica, 9/1/14)

I was born and raised in Hawai'i and I am deeply connected to this place, including the physical environment, the history and its people. A lot of my work in education is motivated by a sense of place, and wanting to give back to this place. (Amber, 9/1/14)

I am a university teacher educator whose practice and research focuses on culturally relevant pedagogy, but deep in my heart would rather be a yoga instructor! This is me, complete with inherent contradictions and multiple identities. (Karen, 9/11/14)

Through this initial sharing about our personal and professional contexts, we started to lay the foundations of not only our international community but also an emergent friendship based on shared values and life experiences.

Ongoing Co-construction of What "We" Mean by Community

The analysis of the data also revealed that an important feature of our community is that it was intellectually and emotionally safe. As the following quote from Jessica illustrates, we saw our community as larger than the total sum of participants.

A community is an aggregate of individual participating members? Nothing more and nothing less? Is there not a sense of community that transcends the participating individuals themselves? The total sum that is larger than everything added up? Isn't this transcendent sense of community what we are working so hard to establish in p4cHI? (Jessica, 11/3/14)

In response to Jessica's entry, Amber added, "It is not just about one particular . . . community of inquiry, but rather about building a more just, caring, empathetic, thoughtful, innovative, civic minded world" (Amber, 11/3/14). As these two quotes illustrate, we thought collectively about what we mean by community and co-constructed our understanding together. This too, helped to cultivate a space where we could truly engage in dialogue, offer constructive feedback, and inquire with one another about what we were interested in and cared about.

Pillar Two: Inquiry

Inquiry was also at the heart of our journaling process. About inquiry, Jackson (2001) writes, "perhaps most basic to successful inquiry is the clear and shared understanding that 'we aren't in a rush to get any-where'" (Jackson, 2001, p. 461). In the context of academic inquiry, *not being in a rush* can take on many meanings. In the case of our journal it meant a number of things.

First it meant that we took the time to pursue, dig deep, and scratch beneath the surface of our scholarly interests. There are many examples in the journal that illustrated how we asked questions about our professional practice and of one another. A quote that illustrates this comes from Mitsuyo. On October 15, 2014 she wrote, "I feel frustrated when students do not look at me. But is it because I was in American graduate school? What is the ideal image of p4c facilitator? Perhaps each of us has a different answer to this question" (10/15/14). In response to Mitsuyo we spent many pages of writing searching for evidence to support our emerging conclusions about the topic of eye contact. As a part of this process we let ourselves pursue tangents that may have seemed unconnected to the topic of the inquiry. Eventually, these inquiries lead us to new realizations.

Another example of how we were not in a rush during our inquiries is found in the journal entries where we took the time to pause and to respond with one another in thoughtful and caring ways. For example, Karen wrote,

> Thanks for your patience everybody! Even though the teachers' strike is still on, impacting deeply on both my personal and professional lives, we are taking each week at a time and hoping for a resolution. So, now I can start my own journaling and add to the thoughtful and insightful comments made so far. (Karen, 9/11/14)

In response to Karen's entry about a four-month strike that kept her and other colleagues away from a profession that they love and the students that they are connected to, Jessica comforted her.

> I have time to write this much because our school semester has not started. It starts on 9/22. So no pressure on other people. In P4C we try to stay as true to life as possible. I felt sorry that Karen's life was affected by the strike. Hope things turn out for the better. (Jessica, 9/10/14)

Despite all of the various elements of our life that we were juggling as professional educators, researchers, mothers, and wives each of us made sure that we were fully present when it came to writing in our journals.

Also related to not being in a rush, in a number of journal entries we saw how the time that we dedicated to our journal writing counterbalanced our frantic and often chaotic lifestyles by giving us a space to breathe and to *be present in the moment.* This was evident in Amber's writing. On September 8, 2014 she wrote,

> Wow! I had to drag myself to the computer this morning, and after reading our journal I am so excited and invigorated about this work! Everyone has helped me reconnect to the "bigger picture" (e.g. working to better humanity, live the good life, cultivate self-reflection, etc.).

Then, on November 3, 2014 she stated, "I am working on how to live a balanced life when life is very full," but I must say, that I "always enjoy returning to the journal. It is like taking a breath of fresh air." This quest to find balance between life and work became a topical theme in our journal; it was woven in-between and throughout the questions and reflections of our academic inquiries. As critical friends, we were mindful of the many obligations and responsibilities that pulled us all in different directions and we allowed ourselves, and one another to include the multiple facets of our lives in our professional inquiry. As a result, our journal was both personally and professionally meaningful.

Pillar Three: Philosophy

In our journaling project, each of us was a *little p* (Jackson, 2012) philosopher. We engaged in the activity of philosophy by raising questions and pursuing our wonderings. As critical friends we were able to respond to these examinations based on our experiences in different cultural contexts. For example, Lulu "questioned what is philosophy," whether it is "about logic" or "the way of life," whether there are "fundamental differences between Western philosophy and Eastern philosophy," or even whether there is "such a notion as 'eastern' and 'western' philosophy" (10/17/14). Jessica wondered about what "counts as a *philosophical* question" and whether the criterion might be anything other than "a genuine wonder" or "a true question in life" (11/10/14)." Karen wanted to know how "philosophical wisdom" relates to "traditional practices of mindfulness and awareness," about "being awake and being intentional" (9/11/14). This spirit of wonderment permeated throughout our journaling exchange.

As critical friends, we also considered and countered one another's arguments. Mindful of the cultural diversity of our contexts we did our best to suspend preconceived ideas and situational biases. In a non-judgmental and respectful way, we challenged one another to justify what constituted a "good" answer to the questions we were pursuing. As a result, we arrived at a number of conclusions that were shaped by the multiple perspectives and interpretations of our international peers.

Pillar Four: Reflection

Participants in p4cHI style inquiries endeavor to reflect upon their lives and their experiences, to confront inherent complexities and conundrums, in order to research for new meanings and transform their experiences. They thoughtfully respond to diverse perspectives/points of view and explore possible connections to deepen the inquiry and enhance self-knowledge. They are able to challenge, modify or correct their own thinking in light of new experiences and new meanings. This interest in reflection is an important reason why we each chose to join the international journaling project in the first place.

As Jessica wrote, "I believe in the power of dialogue and of reflection. And this is a rare opportunity for each of us to embark on an adventure that will eventually amount to something much larger than ourselves" (9/1/14). Lulu also wrote that keeping this journal helped her "reflect on my own experiences" (8/28/14). Admitting that finding time to reflect in the middle of an already busy schedule is difficult Amber wrote, "I am hoping that this project will 'force' me (for lack of a better word) to sit down each week and write/reflect and I love that I am writing to an 'audience' of listeners" (9/1/14).

Self-Correction

Finding the time to reflect upon our experiences provided us with a rare opportunity to step aside from our immediate experiences and look at them in new ways, and in some cases, it provided us with the opportunity to change or self-correct our thoughts about a particular topic. One example of this was Jessica's new realizations about why her students avoided eye contact with each other during class time. In the following quote she demonstrates how she thought through this particular challenge and drew her own conclusion.

> As I reflect upon this class scenario, I thought that "being open" does not mean accepting any viewpoints with no boundaries. Being open means being willing to enter into the worlds the students were experiencing so that I can enter into the dialogue with them. I am curious to know what reality they were experiencing, which is totally different from mine (I had not experienced shyness or nervousness for a long time). Having understood their major concern with shyness, I was then able to move them to their next level of overcoming their shyness by gradually getting used to it and by eventually cultivating a new habit, a new way of being with oneself and the other, and a new way of encountering the world. (Jessica, 10/26/14)

Through reflection and dialogue with the other members of our journaling group, Jessica was able to modify her original assumptions about her students, self-correct, and draw new conclusions about the reasons for her students' behaviors.

Like Jessica, this process of self-reflection and self-correction, enabled all of us to think meta-cognitively about our experiences and find new meanings. Such reflective thinking demonstrated in our journals supported our developing understanding of self, and "about really understanding the other person, integrating different voices, and in the process enlarging one's worldviews" (Jessica, 12/22/14). Such reflection is "not a scientific act aiming at verification of knowledge, but a communicative, artful act aiming at the resolution of tensions or the equilibrium of experiences" (Jessica, 12/22/14).

In summary, the findings that emerged from this most recent analysis of our data helped to develop our thinking about how the four pillars of p4cHI (community, inquiry, philosophy, and reflection) provided us with the framework and tools for co-constructing a community of critical friends who are collectively committed to engaging in a mindful professional practice.

CONCLUSION

At this study's conclusion we found a direct relationship between philosophy for children Hawai'i, critical friendship, and mindfulness. This is seen through the four pillars of p4cHI:

1. *Community* is a fundamental component of critical friendship, which emphasizes identifying and sharing values concerning practice (Samaras, 2011; Schuck and Russell, 2005) as well as developing a climate of trust, compassion and empathy (Ragoonaden and Bullock, 2016). Further by clearly articulating with one another what we meant by a respectful, safe, and caring environment, we consciously modeled elements of mindfulness and attention to the evolving state of our relationships (Meiklejohn et al., 2012). As the findings from our study illustrate, the presence of critical friendship and mindfulness reiterate the importance of creating supportive, empathetic, and non-judgmental contexts in which to improve practice.

2. *Inquiry* that is characterized by "not being in a rush" (Jackson, 2001) is a very important element of mindfulness and critical friendship. Kabat-Zinn (1990) points to the importance of being present in our day to day activities, of taking the time to appreciate, to consider and to be grateful for the day to day, moment to moment activities of our daily lives. In our case, our regular journaling became a safe haven where we could retreat into inquiry with one another. In our inquiries we took the time to reflect, we were present, and we responded to each other in thoughtful and intentional ways. As a result of these mindful interactions with one another, our critical friendship was cultivated and nurtured.

3. *Philosophy* that begins in wonder and leads to spontaneous questions about the world and ourselves is an essential activity for persons who are interested in developing critical friendships and mindful practices. In our attempt to philosophize about what we

know or do not know, we are able to confront our own sense of confusion and "our own situated-ness in the world" (Jackson, 2012, p. 5). Costa and Kallick (1993) address the importance of critical friends asking provocative questions that help us confront what we take for granted. In addition, Swaffield (2007) emphasizes a critical friend's freedom to be intellectually subversive, challenging accepted wisdom and promoting new intellectual paradigms. All of this is connected to the mindful practice of seeing the world through beginner's eyes, which includes allowing our senses to fully embrace an event in a slow, thoughtful, and intentional manner (University of British Columbia, 2015). In our journal we engaged in the activity of "little p" philosophy to cultivate our critical friendships, become more mindful, and live the examined life (Jackson, 2012, p. 5)

4. *Reflection* is inherent in the process of developing critical friendship and mindfulness. Critical friendship is a technique rooted in reflection and analysis. Baskerville and Goldblatt (2007) support the notion that a critical friend is a reflective practitioner who aims to improve practice by challenging a colleague's practice in a safe, nurturing manner. Biggs and Tang (2007) recognized the importance of critical friendship as a process encouraging reflection and mindful improvement. As the results of this study illustrate, the reflection that we engaged in our international online collaborative journaling project helped to mature the emergent qualities of our critical friendships and mindful practice.

SIGNIFICANCE TO THE FUTURE OF OUR INTERNATIONAL ONLINE COLLABORATIVE JOURNALING PROJECT

Framed by the four pillars of philosophy for children Hawai'i, self-study methodologies and online journaling with international partners provided us with a space to learn and grow as critical friends and mindful scholar practitioners. Prior to this study, most of us were aware of the importance of employing critical friendships (Miles and Huberman, 1994) during self-study research, but we had not yet discovered the powerful role that mindfulness plays in carrying out meaningful approaches to S-S-STEP research. This sentiment is echoed by Macintyre Latta, and Buck (2007) who stipulate that "self-study is . . . key to professional development and [should] reflect our desire to do more than 'deliver' courses in teacher education" (p. 189). With its focus on the human capacity for observation, participation, and acceptance of life's moments from a loving, compassionate stance, mindful activity within the context of practitioner research like ours develops deep understandings of context, experiential approaches, and the pursuit of positive change in educational environments. As we move forward, and collectively plan the next stages of our international online collaborative journaling project we will use what we have learned and be more mindful about applying the elements of community, inquiry, philosophy, and reflection to deepen our understanding of self, other, and our professional practice.

REFERENCES

Baskerville, D., and Goldblatt, H. (2009). Learning to be a critical friend: From professional indifference through challenge to unguarded conversations. *Cambridge Journal of Education* 39, no. 2: 205–22. doi: 10.1080/03057640902902260

Beck, C., Freese, A., and Kosnik, C. (2004). The preservice practicum: Learning through self-study in a professional setting. In J. J. Loughran, M. L. Hamilton, V. K. LaBoskey, and T. Russell (Eds.), *International handbook of self-study of teaching and teacher education practices* (pp. 1259–93). Dordrecht: Kluwer.

Biggs, J. B., and Tang, C. S. (2007). *Teaching for quality learning at university: What the student does* (3rd ed.). Maidenhead, UK: McGraw-Hill/Society for Research into Higher Education and Open University Press.

Charmaz, K. (2006). *Constructing grounded theory: A practical guide through qualitative analysis*. Los Angeles, CA: Sage.

Costa, A., and Kallick, B. (1993). Through the lens of a critical friend. *Educational Leadership* 51, no. 2: 49–51.

Creswell, J. W. (2007). *Qualitative inquiry and research design: Choosing among five approaches*. Thousand Oaks, CA: Sage.

Dewey, J. (1916). *Democracy and education*. New York: Macmillan.

Elliott-Johns, S., Peterson, S., Allison-Roan, V., and Ramirez, L. (2010). A cross-continent collaboration: Seeking community to support critical inquiry in teacher education. In L. B. Erickson, J. R. Young, and S. Pinnegar (Eds.), *Navigating the public and private: Negotiating the diverse landscape of teacher education* (pp. 81–84). Provo, UT: Bringham Young University.

Glaser, B. G., and Strauss, A. L. (1967). *The discovery of grounded theory: Strategies for qualitative research*. Chicago: Aldine.

Hultman Özek, Y., Edgren, G., and Jandér, K. (2012). Implementing the critical friend method for peer feedback among teaching librarians in an academic setting. *Evidenced Based Library and Information Practice* 7, no. 4: 68–81. Retrieved from https://ejournals.library.ualberta.ca/index.php/EBLIP/article/view/16600/14564

Jackson. T. (2013). Philosophical rules of engagement. In S. Goering, N. Shudak, and T. Wartenberg (Eds.), *Philosophy in schools: An introduction for philosophers and teachers* (pp. 99–109). New York: Routledge.

Jackson, T. (2012). Home grown. *Educational Perspectives* 44, nos. 1 and 2: 3–7.

Jackson, T. (2001). The art and craft of 'gently Socratic' inquiry. In A. L. Costa (Ed.), *Developing minds: A resource book for teaching thinking* (pp. 459–65). Alexandria, VA: Association for Supervision and Curriculum Development.

Kabat-Zinn, J. (1990). *Full catastrophe living: Using the wisdom of your body and mind to face stress, pain, and illness*. New York: Dell.

Kabat-Zinn, J. (2003). Mindfulness-based interventions in context: Past, present, and future. *Clinical Psychology: Science and Practice* 10: 144–56.

Kosnik, C., Samaras, A. P., and Freese, A. R. (2006). Beginning with trusted friends: Venturing out to work collaboratively in our institutions. In L. Fitzgerald, M. Heston, and D. Tidwell (Eds.), *Collaboration and community: Pushing boundaries* (pp. 152–56). Cedar Falls, IA: University of Northern Iowa. Retrieved from http://resources.educ.queensu.ca/ar/sstep/S-STEP6-2006.pdf.

Lee, O. (2010). Facilitating preservice teachers' reflection through interactive online journal writing. *Physical Educator* 67, no. 3: 128–39.

Loughran, J. (2007). Researching teacher education practices: Responding to the challenges, demands, and expectations of self-study. *Journal of Teacher Education* 58, no. 1: 12–20.

Lukey, B. (2013). A p4c experiment: The high school philosopher in residence. In S. Goering, N. Shudak and T. Wartenberg (Eds.), *Philosophy in schools: An introduction for philosophers and teachers* (pp. 43–55). New York: Routledge.

Lunenberg, M., and Samaras, A. (2011). Developing a pedagogy for teaching self-study research: Lessons learned across the Atlantic. *Teaching and Teacher Education* 27: 841–50. doi:10.1016/j.tate.2011.01.008

Macintyre, L., and Buck, L. (2007). Professional development risks and opportunities embodied within self-study. *Studying Teacher Education* 3, no. 2: 189–205.

Mackenzie, E. (2015). Mindfulness training: A transdisciplinary approach to assessing efficacy in education. In Karen Ragoonaden (Ed.), *Mindful teaching and learning: Developing a pedagogy of well-being* (pp. 1–7). Lanham, MD: Lexington.

Makaiau, A. S. (2015). *Cultivating and Nurturing Collaborative Civic Spaces*. C3 Teachers. Retrieved from http://c3teachers.org/c3shifts.

Makaiau, A. S. (2014). Philosophical inquiry curriculum guide: Course overview, standards and supporting documents. Unpublished manuscript. Uehiro Academy for Philosophy and Ethics in Education, University of Hawai'i at Manoa, Hawai'i, USA.

Makaiau, A. S. (2010). *Adolescent identity exploration in a multicultural community context; An educator's approach to rethinking identity interventions*. Doctoral dissertation, University of Hawai'i at Mänoa, Honolulu, HI.

Makaiau, A. S., Wang, J. Ching-Sze, Ragoonaden, K., and Leng, L. (In press). Empowering global P4C research and practice through self-study: The philosophy for children Hawai'i international journaling and self-study project. In M. Gregory, J. Haynes, and K. Murris (Eds.), *International handbook of Philosophy for Children*. New York: Routledge.

Makaiau, A. S., Leng, L., and Fukui, S. (2015). Journaling and self-study in an international research collective. *Studying Teacher Education* 11, no. 1: 64–80.

Makaiau, A. S., and Freese, A. R. (2013). A transformational journey: Exploring our multicultural identities through self-study. *Studying Teacher Education* 9, no. 2: 141–51.

Makaiau, A. S., and Miller, C. (2012). The philosopher's pedagogy. *Educational Perspectives, 44*, 8–19.

Meiklejohn, J., Phillips, C., Freedman, M.L., Griffin, M. L, Biegel, G., Roach, A., Frank, J., Burke, C., Pinger, L., Soloway, G., Isberg, R., Sibinga, E., Grossman, L., and Saltzman, A. (2012). Integrating mindfulness training into K–12 education: Fostering the resilience of students and teachers. *Mindfulness* 3: 291–307.

Miles, M. B., and Huberman, A. M. (1994). *Qualitative data analysis* (2nd ed.). Thousand Oaks, CA: Sage Publications.

Ord, W. (2016). *Introduction to mindfulness*. Retrieved from http://thinkingeducation.co.uk/courses-training

Plato. (1938/1961). In E. Hamilton and H. Cairns (Eds.), *The collected dialogues of Plato: Including the letters*. Princeton, NJ: Princeton University Press.

Poulin, P. A., Mackenzie, C. S., Soloway, G., and Karaoylas, E. C. (2008). Mindfulness training as an evidenced-based approach to reducing stress and promoting well-being among human services professionals. *International Journal of Health Promotion and Education* 46: 72–80.

Ragoonaden, K. (2015). *Mindful teaching and learning: Developing a pedagogy of well-being*. Lanham, MD: Lexington.

Ragoonaden, K., and Bullock, S. M. (2016). Critical Friends: The Practiced Wisdom of Professional Development. In K. Ragoonaden and S. Bullock (Eds), *Mindfulness and critical friendship: A new perspective on professional development for educators* (pp. 13–32). Lanham, MD: Lexington.

Samaras, A. P. (2011). Self-study teacher research: Improving your practice through collaborative inquiry. Thousand Oaks, CA: Sage

Samaras, A. P., and Freese, A. R. (2006). *Self-study of teaching practices.* New York: Peter Lang.

Samaras, A., Hicks, M., and Garvey Berger, J. (2004). Self-study through personal history. In J. Loughran, M.-L. Hamilton, V. K. LaBoskey, and T. Russell. (Eds), *International handbook of self-study of teaching and teacher education practice* (pp. 817–69). Dordrecht, The Netherlands: Springer.

Schön, D. A. (1983). *The reflective practitioner: How professionals think in action.* London: Temple Smith.

Schön, D. A. (1987). *Educating the reflective practitioner.* San Francisco, CA: Jossey-Bass.

Schuck, S., and Russell, T. (2005). Self-study, critical friendship, and the complexities of teacher education. *Studying Teacher Education* 1, no. 2: 107–21.

Sheets, R. H. (2005). *Diversity pedagogy: Examining the role of culture in the teaching-learning process.* Boston, MA: Pearson.

Strauss, A., and Corbin, J. (1998). *Basics of qualitative research: Techniques and procedures for developing grounded theory.* Thousand Oaks, CA: Sage.

Swaffield, S. (2007). Light touch critical friendship. *Improving Schools* 10, no. 3: 205–19.

University of British Columbia (UBC). (2015). Smart Education Facilitator Manual.

SIX

Critical Friendship and Meta-Critical Friendship

Reinterrogating Assumptions

Déirdre Ní Chróinín, Mary O'Sullivan, and Tim Fletcher

This chapter shares the experiences of three physical education teacher educators (Déirdre and Mary based in Ireland and Tim based in Canada) as we collaborated to develop and implement new pedagogical approaches in our teacher education programs. We were inspired by compelling theoretical arguments in favor of prioritizing meaningful experiences in PE and coaching settings (Kretchmar, 2000; 2005; 2008). In the absence of empirical evidence we sought to build a set of physical education teacher education (PETE) pedagogies that support pre-service teachers' learning how to facilitate meaningful physical activity experiences in physical education which we called LAMPE (Learning About Meaningful Physical Education). Scott Kretchmar's work informed our identification of criteria for meaningful experience in PE: challenge, social interaction, increased motor competence, fun and delight (Kretchmar, 2000; 2001; 2006).

We adopted a Self-Study of Teacher Education practices (S-STEP) methodological frame to gain insight on and interrogate our experiences of developing and implementing LAMPE. Researching one's own teacher education practices is acknowledged as a landmark professional development activity for teacher educators (Loughran, 2014). By initiating development of LAMPE through an S-STEP frame—which is improvement-aimed (LaBoskey, 2004)—we implicitly committed to investing in our own professional learning and development as teacher educators. In identifying a clear and explicit focus on the self-in-practice (Ovens and Fletcher, 2014; Pinnegar and Hamilton, 2009) we were conscious, however, of the perspective that 'personal practice develops in tandem with a practitioner's beliefs and images of appropriate practices and thus tends to be comfortable' (Schuck and Russell 2005 p. 108). In recognition that personal and professional growth often requires moving out of our comfort zones, we built multiple interactions with peers/critical friends into the design of our research (Pinnegar and Hamilton, 2009). We anticipated opportunities for our own professional learning through sharing and discussion of our teacher education practices. LaBoskey (2004) suggests that interactivity in self-study is crucial because "garnering multiple perspectives on our professional practice settings helps to challenge our assumptions and biases, reveal our inconsistencies, expand our potential interpretations, and triangulate our findings" (p. 849). We used critical friendship to support and challenge (Schuck and Russell, 2005) our beliefs and practices as we developed and implemented LAMPE. The critical friend role was intended to be a "trusted person who asks provocative questions, provides data to be examined through another lens, and offers critique of a person's work as a friend" (Costa and Kallick, 1993, p. 50). Mindfulness was not the starting point for our research but there are certainly aspects of our self-study, particularly related to the processes of critical friendship, that resonate with benefits associated with mindfulness including increased self-awareness and regulation of attention (Hölzel et al., 2011). This chapter outlines how our learning was supported by a three-way critical friendship (Déirdre, Tim, and Mary) as we developed, implemented and researched LAMPE.

Across a two-year period (2013–2015) Tim and Déirdre experimented with Learning About Meaningful Physical Education (LAMPE) as a pedagogical practice with undergraduate classes in Canada and Ireland, respectively. Déirdre implemented LAMPE with generalist elementary teachers in an introductory Physical Education course. Prospective specialist PE teachers and coaches experienced LAMPE in a Developmental Games course led by Tim. The first level of critical friendship was between Tim and Déirdre who interacted through sharing weekly reflective journal entries and engaged in regular recorded Skype conversations. The weekly reflections were framed by questions which we designed to push us to uncomfortable places: *How/when was I made to feel vulnerable during the lesson? How did I handle this?* We also encouraged the critical friend to be conscious of their "critical" role by using prompts to respond, for example: *What resonated with my thinking was . . . , The questions that it raised for me are . . . ,* and *If I was going to be contentious I might suggest . . .* At the end of each of the four teaching semesters we identified "turning points" (Bullock and Ritter, 2011) which we shared initially with each other.

The second level of critical friendship involved a type of "meta-critical friend" that offered an additional layer of critical engagement. We selected Mary for this role as she is a world-renowned and vastly experienced PETE practitioner and researcher. We anticipated that her breadth of knowledge and expertise and her range of experience of PETE practices would enhance the development of LAMPE. We also hoped that Mary would keep us on track, helping to solve problems as they arose, supporting and guiding us through uncertainties as well as critiquing our approach in ways that would make LAMPE robust and of high quality. Mary did this by reviewing our end-of-semester "turning points" documents and responded by inserting comments and questions. She also participated in three-way dialogues (mostly on Skype) with Déirdre and Tim about aspects of LAMPE including a review of progress, design of next steps and dissemination of findings. In the following sections we share the experience of Déirdre and Tim acting as critical friends to each other and also Mary's experience of the "meta-critical friend" role. We highlight the value of peer interaction and support in developing, implementing, researching and enhancing pedagogical practices and the personal and professional benefits for teacher educators that result.

Déirdre and Tim's Perspective

Thornburg (2007) identifies four archetypal learning spaces:

- The campfire, a place for storytellers and experts to share wisdom
- The waterhole, a place for peer sharing and learning
- The cave, a place where the learner is alone allowing for individual study and reflection.
- "Life," where all knowledge is tested and refined through application

Adapting Thornburg's metaphor to teacher educator professional learning spaces might look like this: The cave, a space for individual study and reflection, is where teacher educators spend a significant portion of their learning time, reading, reviewing, and writing. The watering hole, a space for incidental meetings and small group discourse and collaboration with peers, is visited by teacher educators over coffee with colleagues, in reading groups, and in program committees. Teacher educators rarely, however, discuss the detail of their own individual teacher educator practices at the waterhole. The campfire is a place for storytelling, sharing of expert knowledge and large group discussion that is rarely accessible to teacher educators. Teacher education conferences and sharing events offer teacher educators opportunities to spend time at the campfire. The "life" learning space acknowledges the learning that happens for teacher educators in the ordinary enactment of their daily teacher education practices where they learn through application working with pre-service teacher education candidates. In many cases this latter learning space reflects incidental and trial and error learning rather than formal intentional planned teacher educator learning. Given that most teacher educators spend more time in "life" than in the other learning spaces, this is the space that has probably the greatest influence on teacher education practices.

Before the Learning About Meaningful Physical Education (LAMPE) project Tim had engaged in critical friendships previously so he was practiced at the processes of sharing his practice and commenting on others' practices. Déirdre, on the other hand, had rarely left the cave before. A collaborative approach to developing, implementing and re-searching LAMPE positioned the waterhole as a prioritized space for our teacher educator learning related to LAMPE. The design of the research project involved moving from the "life" learning space where we enacted LAMPE pedagogies to the waterhole space where we discussed and ana-lyzed these experiences. While we returned to the cave intermittently we did not spend prolonged periods of time in isolation—our simultaneous development and researching of LAMPE pedagogies demanded regular interaction to share decisions, problems, questions and discoveries we made during weekly "life" space teaching and learning experiences.

Our critical friendship processes of sharing our practices on a weekly basis provided a structure that placed our learning about the pedagogies of teacher educators at the forefront of our attention and made us "lmind-ful" of our teacher education practices. For the purposes of this chapter we adopt an understanding of mindfulness as a psychological state of raised awareness in relation to specific aspects of our teacher education practices, in this case, LAMPE. Identification of an explicit research ques-tion related to our teacher education practices demanded an increased level of noticing related to our implementation of LAMPE pedagogies. Mindfulness, which has its origins in ancient Buddhist practices, is often associated with sitting in stillness with eyes closed with a focus on non-judgemental awareness in the present moment (Hölzel et al., 2011). As physical educators we did not, however, sit or stay still, but rather used critical friendship to help us to act in implementing LAMPE supported by reflection with a critical friend. Our interactions as critical friends helped us to sustain our focus (Hölzel et al., 2011). For example, in one reflective journal entry, Déirdre said:

> I have found the quality of interaction and support from Tim to be particularly valuable in supporting my implementation of the [LAMPE] approach. On reflection, without Tim my approach would not have been the same. I honestly do not think I would have achieved the same results without Tim, in fact I am not even sure I would have had the conviction to persevere—not because I was not convinced of the approach but because change is always challenging (Déirdre, end of year reflection, Year 1).

Critical friendship helped us (Tim and Déirdre) to persist with developing and implementing LAMPE. Our commitment to regular interactions through e-mail and skype provided a framework that helped us to maintain a specific focus on LAMPE and avoid distractions in our busy teacher educator lives. There was accountability in the knowledge that the critical friend was waiting on a weekly reflection to arrive in his/her e-mail inbox, which ensured a present moment prioritisation of LAMPE research processes. In this way the processes of critical friendship acted as an accountability mechanism to persist with the innovation that pushed us to overcome obstacles and uncertainties in our practice. Through regular sharing of teacher education experiences we developed resilience. For example, it was acceptable for plans to go awry:

> You are right Deirdre. These are my assumptions and I should be trying to get some evidence in some form or another. Thanks for the push to go beyond my own view of this—I think I needed the nudge (Tim, reflection 4, Year 1)

We viewed problems we encountered as opportunities to develop our understanding rather than obstacles:

> Sharing my teaching through the written reflections and bouncing ideas around on Skype were critical in figuring things out when I got stuck and keeping me on track when my focus was fuzzy or direction unclear (Déirdre, end of year reflection, Year 1).

Similar to findings found with pre-service teachers (Meiklejohn et al., 2012), mindful reflection on particular experiences related to LAMPE helped us to reframe experiences that we might have initially considered failures and roadblocks as surmountable challenges. Viewing obstacles in more positive ways increased our resilience to failure and supported us to innovate into new spaces. Critical friendship ensured we were not isolated or alone in engaging with LAMPE development. We acknowledge that the innovation would not have continued without regular visits to the waterhole learning space (for Skype discussions, e-mails and meetings) for support, guidance and the friendship that grew as we collaborated to develop LAMPE in our "life" learning space of PETE practices.

Teaching can be a "vulnerable act, performed at the dangerous intersection of the public and the personal" (Palmer, 2010, p. 3). Adopting a new and untested pedagogical approach involved a level of risk and vulnerability with the students we teach. Vulnerability is also an important component of S-STEP methodologies; based on a willingness to interrogate and make judgements of ourselves, and an openness to perhaps change one's ideas and/or practices as a result (Hamilton and Pinnegar, 2000). Given our aim to reframe our teacher education practices through creation and refinement of a new teacher education pedagogy, our commitment to S-STEP methodology necessitated a critique and interaction with peers on our pedagogies. Sharing of practices held the potential to "demonstrate our integrity by bringing together our beliefs and actions" (Hamilton and Pinnegar, 2000, p. 239) but could also highlight inconsistencies in our practices. Our vulnerability index was heightened given that peers may be more discerning than the students in relation to teaching competence and knowledge of curriculum. In recognizing that we teach who we are (Palmer, 2010) an awareness of our weaknesses as well as our strengths and openness to the possibility/desirability of personal as well as professional growth became central to our self-study processes. Vulnerability was an inevitable, and we suggest essential, aspect of our critical friendship as we together worked to develop and implement LAMPE. We had no blueprint to follow and were dependent on each other to guide our approach. We had no choice but to admit our uncertainties and to ask questions for which we had no answers. We approached the sharing process in a spirit of openness that reflected our desire to learn and to improve our teacher education practices. At the end of year 1 Déirdre reflected:

> Looking back on the whole pilot [project] I actually now believe that the process itself of adopting and implementing this approach made me vulnerable. I was probably vulnerable every week, in every lecture because there was no manual to follow and much of my planning involved interpreting the work of Kretchmar and applying it to practice (and hoping I was on the right track) (Déirdre, end of year reflection, Year 1).

We suggest that a willingness to risk being vulnerable in making mistakes and acknowledging a lack of expertise was a necessary prerequisite of developing LAMPE as both an authentic and realistic approach to supporting pre-service teachers' and coaches learning. We needed to expose our doubts in order to open up alternative ways of being a teacher educator and doing teacher education. Being mindful of our own feelings about our teaching experiences provided a starting point for discussions that might not otherwise have happened.

Engaging with our thoughts and feelings about our teacher education practices and paying attention to our "self" helped us to develop a more consistent teacher educator approach by identifying principles of our respective practices. Naming and then sharing these principles with each other, and finding resonance in each other's positions, resulted in feelings of authenticity as well as a more nuanced self-understanding in practice. Tim acknowledged the feeling associated with coming to such understanding: *"It is almost like an epiphany to be able to really hang your hat on something"* (Tim, end of year reflection, Year 1). As a result of this heightened understanding, we were better positioned to act from a place of greater awareness of our values and priorities as teacher educators. Moving between the waterhole and "life" learning spaces helped direct our energies to living through our teaching the values we held about meaningful physical education and how best to support our students to learn to facilitate meaningful experiences in physical activity settings. A feeling of authenticity resulted from the alignment of our pedagogies and these values which further reinforced our pedagogical "self" through congruent actions.

Mary was the third participant in this three-way critical friendship. The term "meta-critical friend" which we now use to describe her role did not exist at the outset of this project. The term was coined by Renee Clift, who served as discussant for the session in which we first presented our research about LAMPE pedagogies at the American Educational Research Association conference in Chicago in April 2015 (which also serves as evidence of learning within the campfire learning space). We have adopted the term "meta-critical friend" ever since as we felt it effectively represented Mary's position as a subject expert and her distance from the everyday implementation of the research project. In terms of the learning spaces outlined above, Mary met us occasionally at the waterhole to interact. She did not come to the waterhole for idle conversation, however. Mary added an extra layer of criticality and value to the process of LAMPE development by adopting both a supportive and critical role simultaneously. Mary's critical role was evident when she challenged our assumptions by interrogating our written responses, asking "so what" questions and demanding more evidence to support our claims. For example:

> This is a really interesting commentary as far as it goes. What I would like to know and perhaps for Deirdre to make explicit to herself as well as Tim is what aspects of her thinking are being challenged. What approaches to your teaching do you now see in some more problematic ways . . . and why . . . and what are you thinking would need to change and why . . . this gets at the deeper meanings/understandings of your positioning and view on [LAMPE] teaching and should make it more obvious the actions that are needed/ or the change of values that have been clarified (Mary, comment on turning points, Year 1).

Mary also input on the overall development of LAMPE. In particular, she helped us to overcome challenges in LAMPE development. She also provided a sounding board for our ideas which was important as there was little literature to refer to for guidance. In her supportive role Mary's encouragement increased our confidence in the value of developing LAMPE and assured us that we were "on track."

> You have something here but (and yes I am very much in a mode of critical friend here) there are issues . . . You need to be more persuasive to bring me on board . . . you have an idea but you have to sell me on it (Mary, e-mail correspondence, Year 2).

Below Mary shares her experience of acting as a "meta-critical friend" to Déirdre and Tim in this research.

Mary's Perspective as a "Meta-Critical Friend"

I have worked for over twenty-five years as a physical education teacher educator. My research interests revolve around the policies, politics, and practices (Cochran-Smith, 2006) of teacher education and teachers' professional development. At the time of my engagement with the Learning About Meaningful Physical Education project I was serving as a senior university administrator and I was somewhat removed from the daily practice of teacher education. I was committed to supporting the research agendas of my younger colleagues where I could. I had worked previously with Déirdre on a number of PETE research projects but my interactions with Tim were more limited. His commitment to building an S-STEP research network around pedagogies of Physical Education teaching and coach education addresses an important gap in the PETE literature. I was keen to support the distinctive approach to learning to teach physical education that Tim and Déirdre proposed. While many scholars have proposed a more joyful and meaningful (rather than utilitarian) engagement with Physical Education, there has been a paucity of research on the pedagogies of such an approach. I was attracted to the possibility of exploring and developing new evidence-based ways of thinking about PETE learning to teach prospective Physical Education teachers and how this might be understood by other teacher educators. I viewed S-STEP as potentially making an important contribution to a refocusing on pedagogies of PETE and was keen to see how a three-way dialogue (with one person more distanced from the practice) might generate a learning community focused on developing teacher education pedagogies.

When Tim and Deirdre approached me to join the project I understood my task was to ask provocative questions of their research idea, examine their assumptions about this work, confront realities of the workplace and how we were capturing the essence of the principles of LAMPE as a pedagogical approach to learning to teach Physical Education. In reality, I was removed from the day to day implementation of LAMPE pedagogical practices in both countries. While Tim and Déirdre engaged weekly during the semester by sharing written reflections, I engaged with both of them only once a semester as a "meta-critical friend." At the end of teaching semester Tim and Déirdre wrote individual "turning points" in which they identified key critical incidents as to how the semester's experiences had assisted them to better understand aspects of developing and implementing LAMPE pedagogies. These summarized their key learnings from either implementing LAMPE with a cohort of pre-service students or from responding to the reflections of the pedagogical implementer that semester. They each shared three "turning points" for each semester. In turn, I reviewed these documents and shared my responses to these reflections with both of them. We then met in person or on Skype to discuss the issues that arose from our collective writings. These meetings informed the design of the next phase of the study and allowed us to collectively refine the focus of our investigation for the next semester. Reflecting back on my experience as a "meta-critical friend" it is clear that I took up a variety of positions within the three-way conversations and in the written comments on the "turning points" I shared. Below, I describe in more detail the three main positions I adopted in the "meta-critical friend" role.

Firstly, my distance from implementing Learning About Meaningful Physical Education gave me an outsider perspective that resulted in me acting as a *connector of ideas*. I found myself acting as a sounding board for their ideas in ways that allowed me to help Déirdre and Tim make connections between their individual experiences. Starting from their own "turning point" writings I encouraged Déirdre and Tim to make sense of their experiences and draw out the significance and implications of their research for a wider PETE community. Given their immersion in the research process I found my positioning outside of the immediate research process allowed me to scaffold Déirdre's and Tim's thinking and help them to gain a broader perspective on the research. This helped to provide direction for the research design across semesters. For example, together we identified the research question for year 2 and developed the data collection tools to answer the research question:

> This is a very good point. The focus perhaps needs to explicitly shift to thinking about how/when examples of pedagogy are examples of LAMPE (Mary, Tim turning points, Semester 2, Year 2).

My position as a *connector of ideas* would not have been possible without the distance between me and LAMPE implementation.

Secondly, I found myself in the position of *interrogator*. In a number of our meetings, I was in a catch up mode, asking clarifying questions that helped me to understand what Déirdre and Tim were doing. In three-way conversations Tim and Déirdre asked lots of questions to gain support for their approach. I often answered their question with a question. I asked questions to push Deirdre and Tim to explore assumptions in relation to their experiences of implementing LAMPE as I had perceived in their writings. I asked questions that required them to articulate principles of practice on which they based their approach. My outsider status allowed me to probe in ways that would not be possible if I was more involved:

> . . . And I wanted to know what you (both!) understood were the pieces of the puzzle. . . . Nice metaphor but as the outsider I want to know

what the pieces are and what the whole puzzle should reflect (look like-be about) (Mary, Déirdre, turning points, Semester 1, Year 1).

Through questioning and discussion they explored alignment of their teaching practices to the values and commitments of the LAMPE approach. I was conscious of challenging them to position their research within the wider literature on the pedagogies of teacher education. For example:

> Why have you both asked this question? Perhaps we might talk about the relationship if any between pedagogies and content? (Mary, Déirdre, turning point, Semester 1, Year 2).

A challenge as a "meta-critical friend" was in commenting on the pedagogies Déirdre and Tim enacted in their respective teaching spaces as I had not observed, nor had I been invited to observe their teaching. I saw no reason to push for this closer engagement with the project, particularly given their stated vulnerability around how they were trying to implement the pedagogies. While I found my connector position was enhanced by distance from LAMPE implementation I get that sense that the *interrogator* position may benefit from direct observation of LAMPE implementation. While this may not be as helpful in the early stages of development of an innovation it merits consideration as confidence is increased in the pedagogies of the innovation and the teacher educators are more confident in their approach.

Finally, the third position I adopted was as a *mediator*. While I had anticipated from the outset that my role would be critical, a form of quality control of the research, I had not anticipated how I might be called upon to mediate the research relationship between Déirdre and Tim. They had never worked together before (and in fact had never met) so initially they were both tentative and very polite in their interactions. I affirmed their support of each other:

> This then speaks to the value of critical reflection WITH a critical friend . . . (Mary, Déirdre, turning points, Year 1, Semester 1).

While being affirming, at the end of year one I challenged them to examine the nature of their interactions. I prompted them to consider what might be lost in avoiding controversy. I encouraged them to push the boundaries of what was possible in how they acted as critical friends to each other. Drawing on Fullan's (1993) notion of teacher change, my prompting gave Tim and Déirdre permission to move beyond the politeness of their early interactions to critical interrogation of each other's practices and thinking. Different combinations and emphases of the *connector, interrogator*, and *mediator* positions were evident in our interactions as the project developed. In our three-way interactions I adjusted my level of support and critique as it became clear what Déirdre and Tim needed from the "meta-critical friend" role in a given moment. There were also aspects of my role that Déirdre and Tim have shared in conversation that I was not as aware of but merit consideration in selection of a "meta-critical friend." My experience as a teacher educator gave confidence to my two colleagues that they were on the right track in developing the innovation. Also, on a few occasions my advice helped them to overcome obstacles that might have become sticking points, highlighting the value of selecting a "meta-critical friend" with an expertise in the cognate area being examined. I also benefited from my involvement in this research in a number of ways. Through rich focused interactions with professional colleagues I had the opportunity to refresh my thinking on the pedagogies of teacher education in general and PETE in particular. As a senior academic I valued the opportunity to contribute to the field by nurturing physical education scholars and promoting a critical and considered approach to PETE and research of PETE practices.

CONCLUSION

Thornburg's (2007) archetypal learning spaces provide a useful frame for us to talk about our learning experiences within this research. Our experience of three-way critical friendship highlights the value of the waterhole learning space that prioritises peer interaction in supporting our learning as teacher educators. Interactions in the waterhole learning space supported development of Learning About Meaningful Physical Education pedagogies and their successful implementation in the "life" learning space through a "mindful" awareness and interrogation of this specific aspect of our teacher education practices. Researching our experiences through collaborative S-STEP provided a structure that prioritized learning at the waterhole that would not have happened otherwise. In addition, the inclusion of a subject-expert "meta-critical friend" at the waterhole learning space supported development of an innovation in our pedagogical practices. Selection of a critical friend is often determined by project collaborators and their level of expertise may be of relative importance. We suggest that expertise and experience in the given area are essential in the "meta-critical friend" role. Interaction with both our critical friend and "meta-critical friend" helped us to keep focused on our learning goal, supported us to overcome obstacles as they arose and leverage the professional learning opportunities provided to become better teacher educators. In developing the LAMPE pedagogy, it was important that the both Tim and Deidre took time to consider how their approaches were supported by theoretical concepts related to LAMPE as well as how they aligned with their beliefs as teacher educators. Tim and Déirdre were uniquely positioned to provide support as critical friends to each other given that they were both implementing LAMPE pedagogies for the first time. They paid attention to the "right here, right now" by investing in the present moment processes of their pedagogical practices (Tremmel, 1993). The shared novelty of the implementation process allowed them to relate and empathize in ways that that allowed for a shared vulnerability and openness to honest reflection. This authentic voice provided a perspective outside their own that helped Tim and Déirdre to come to understand their practice anew in ways that would not have been possible through self-reflection alone. This shared reflection-*in*-action by Tim and Déirdre was complimented and enhanced by a process of reflection-*on*-action that was facilitated by Mary's distance from the implementation of LAMPE. This combination of action and reflection on multiple levels resulted not only in a reframing of our own teacher education practices, but also creates the potential for us to contribute to the scholarship of teacher education by how we transform our own private theory into public theory grounded in evidence of practice (Hamilton and Pinnegar, 2000; Loughran, 2014). As we enact our teacher education practices in the 'life' learning space we continue to learn alone in the cave learning space and to share our research at the campfire learning space. This research has highlighted to us that aspects of teacher educator professional learning are best pursued in collaboration. We contend that critical friendship and self-study offered a powerful means to encourage innovative pedagogical practices—to change us as teacher educators as well as our practices.

REFERENCES

Baskerville, Delia, and Goldblatt, Helen. (2009). Learning to be a critical friend: From professional indifference through challenge to unguarded conversations. *Cambridge Journal of Education* 39, no. 2: 205–21.

Bullock, Shawn Michael, and Ritter, Jason K. (2011). Exploring the transition into academia through collaborative self-study. *Studying Teacher Education* 7, no. 2: 171–81.

Cochran-Smith, Marilyn. (2006). *Policy, Practice, and Politics in Teacher Education*: Sage.

Costa, Arthur L, and Kallick, Bena. (1993). Through the lens of a critical friend. *Educational leadership, 51*, 49–51.

Fullan, Michael. (1993). *Change forces: Probing the depths of educational reform*. New York: Routledge.

Hamilton, Mary Lynn, and Pinnegar, Stefinee. (2000). On the Threshold of a New Century: Trustworthiness, Integrity, and Self-Study in Teacher Education. *Journal of Teacher Education* 51, no. 3: 234–40.

Hölzel, Britta K., Lazar, Sara W., Gard, Tim, Schuman-Olivier, Zev, Vago, David R., and Ott, Ulrich. (2011). How Does Mindfulness Meditation Work? Proposing Mechanisms of Action From a Conceptual and Neural Perspective. *Perspectives on Psychological Science* 6, no. 6: 537–59.

Kretchmar, R. Scott. (2008). The Increasing Utility of Elementary School Physical Education: A Mixed Blessing and Unique Challenge. *The Elementary School Journal* 108, no. 3: 161–70.

Kretchmar, R. Scott. (2006). Ten more reasons for quality physical education. *Journal of Physical Education, Recreation and Dance* 77, no. 9: 6–9.

Kretchmar, R. Scott. (2005). *Practical Philosophy of Sport and Physical Activity*. Champaign, IL: Human Kinetics.

Kretchmar, R. Scott. (2001). Duty, Habit, and Meaning: Different Faces of Adherence. *Quest* 53, no. 3: 318–25.

Kretchmar, R. Scott. (2000). Movement Subcultures: Sites for Meaning. *Journal of Physical Education, Recreation and Dance* 71, no. 5: 19–25.

LaBoskey, Vicki Kubler. (2004). The methodology of self-study and its theoretical underpinnings *International handbook of self-study of teaching and teacher education practices* (pp. 817–69). Dordrecht, The Netherlands: Springer.

Loughran, John. (2014). Professionally developing as a teacher educator. *Journal of Teacher Education* 65, no. 4: 271–83.

Meiklejohn, J., Phillips, C., Freedman, M.L., Griffin, M. L, Biegel, G., Roach, A., Frank, J., Burke, C., Pinger, L., Soloway, G., Isberg, R., Sibinga, E., Grossman, L., and Saltzman, A. (2012). Integrating mindfulness training into K–12 education: Fostering the resilience of students and teachers. *Mindfulness* 3: 291–307.

Miles, M. B., and Huberman, A. M. (1994). *Qualitative data analysis* (2nd ed.). Thousand Oaks, CA: Sage Publications.

Ovens, Alan, and Fletcher, Tim. (Eds.). (2014). *Self-Study in Physical Education Teacher Education: Exploring the interplay of practice and scholarship (e-book)* Dordrecht, The Netherlands: Springer.

Palmer, Parker J. (2010). *The courage to teach: Exploring the inner landscape of a teacher's life*. Seattle, WA: John Wiley and Sons.

Pinnegar, Stefinee E, and Hamilton, Mary Lynn. (2009). *Self-study of practice as a genre of qualitative research: Theory, methodology, and practice* (Vol. 8) Dordrecht, The Netherlands: Springer Science and Business Media.

Schuck, Sandy, and Russell, Tom. (2005). Self-Study, Critical Friendship, and the Complexities of Teacher Education. *Studying Teacher Education, 1*(2), 107–21.

Thornburg, D. D. (2007). Campfires in Cyberspace: Primordial Metaphors for Learning in the 21st Century. http://tcpd.org/Thornburg/Handouts/Campfires.pdf.

Tremmel, R. (1993). Zen and the art of reflective practice in teacher education. *Harvard Educational Review* 63, no. 4: 434–59.

SEVEN

Cultivating a Mindfulness for McMindfulness

Chris Gilham

Mindfulness In Education (MIE), it could be argued, is one of today's most popular educational topics, in scholarly, professional, and mainstream literature.[1] [2] There is a growing body of evidence supporting mindfulness in education (Burke, 2010; Ergas, 2014; Huppert and Johnson, 2010; Hyland, 2015a; Jennings, Lantieri, and Roeser, 2012; MacKenzie, 2015; McDonald and Shirley, 2009; Meiklejohn et al., 2012; Olsen, 2014; Roeser et al., 2012; Rotne and Rotne, 2013; Ragoonaden, 2015). It is now found in schools throughout North America. Concomitantly, it is increasingly a topic of study in teacher education (Benn et al., 2012, Beshai et al., 2015; Flook et al., 2013; Gold et al., 2010; Jennings et al., 2011; Jennings et al., 2013; Mañas, Franco and Justo, 2011; Metis Associates, 2011; Napoli, 2004; Roeser et al., 2013; Taylor et al., 2015).

For example, MIE is taught as a graduate level course in the School of Education at St. Francis Xavier University (StFX). As a topic of graduate study, it is important for students to be aware of and understand some of the many scholarly discussions on Mindfulness. Most literature extols the benefits and increasing evidence in support of MIE. However, critical discussions are occurring which question the various ways Mindfulness is being taken up in the West. Emergent literature is describing Mindfulness untethered from its historical, Eastern systems of thought as "McMindfulness" (Hyland, 2015b; Purser, 2015; Purser and Loy, 2013)

In this chapter I will explain the context and structure of this graduate course, including a brief introduction and analysis of "McMindfulness" in the context of MIE. In doing so I hope to reveal how the course structure, content and facilitation demonstrated an open yet discerning mindfulness. In conclusion, I will share the results of a post-course research project where I asked students about the possible impacts the MIE course had on their personal and professional lives.

THE STFX UNIVERSITY'S MASTER OF EDUCATION IN LEADERSHIP WITH A FOCUS ON MENTAL HEALTH EDUCATION

Saint Francis Xavier University in Antigonish, Nova Scotia, offered its first graduate level course in Mindfulness in Education (MIE) in the summer of 2014. This course is embedded within a specialized 12-course Masters of Education in Leadership with a focus on Mental Health Education. This degree uses a cohort model, comprised of approximately 20 students, all typically working full time as educators, mainly in Nova Scotia. The students complete all courses together over two years. The goals for our graduate program are:

- To develop future leaders to improve education
- To prepare leaders for educational change
- To engage in critical reflection
- To challenge assumptions and introduce new thinking
- To cultivate educational inquirers and researchers.

Our first Mental Health Education cohort began in the summer of 2014. This cohort will graduate in the summer of 2016, having successfully completed six core leadership focused courses and, another six courses directly related to Mental Health Education such as Restorative Practices, Trauma-informed Practices and, Social Emotional Learning. Mindfulness in Education (MIE) is one of the latter six courses. MIE is a three-credit, thirty-six-hour course. In the summer of 2015 I had the privilege of facilitating this course for this cohort. The course was taught face to face on campus, during the last two weeks of July. Students were also given the option to participate synchronously online, from their homes.

In the course students explored and engaged in mindfulness practices, as well as research related to mindfulness in P–12 settings. Students also explored critical readings of mindfulness. These readings demanded careful attention to what is culturally and sociologically produced, or concealed, in current efforts to embrace mindfulness. Through this three-pronged approach, students continued to examine their identities, practices, and professional contexts. The course is structured through the following questions:

1. What does it mean to practice and be "mindful"?
2. What is the complex history of mindfulness?
3. What thinking and practices have been involved in the nascent history of MIE?

4. How are these histories and practices intertwined with our current attitudes, knowledge, and skills as educators?
5. How might MIE support living well with and for one another in education?
6. What kind of attitudes, knowledge, and skills will I embrace as a result of this course?

In the cohort model instructors typically spend considerable time and energy community building. At the time of the course, the cohort had already taken seven courses together. Additionally, I had already taught two courses to this cohort, including the first mandatory course for all Faculty of Education graduate students at StFX. The first course is on anti-oppression education and the sociological contexts of schooling. In this course students unpack the common culture of meritocracy and see the power and privileges inherent to a colonized education system. Students learn about poverty, the colonization of Canada's Indigenous and African populations, LGBTQ, the gender binary, the hyper-sexualization of women and girls, and the Social Determinants of Health. Critical media literacy is also taught. A great deal of unlearning takes place as students are asked to continuously reflect on their own educational timelines. A final assignment requires them to unpack their student experiences in schools. This unlearning requires thoughtful community building so that students build trust among their peers (and the instructor) and, feel safe to engage in this important self-work.

In these ways, according to the literature, the cohort model cultivates Critical Friendships (Andreu et al., 2003; Bambino, 2002; Butler, 2011; Costa and Kallik, 1993; Swaffield, 2002, 2003, 2004, 2007, 2008; Storey, 2013). Ongoing dialogue between students on important, contentious, and highly politicized topics is nurtured through community circles, stop-start-continue like activities, and various challenge assignments, for examples. Our cohort model is inherently "measured against the core critical friendship characteristics of trust, provocative questioning, alternative perspective, constructive critique and advocacy" (Swaffield, 2008, p. 328).

Also, inherent in the success of our cohort model is the balance between "friend" and "critic" (MacBeath, 1998) and a relationship that is neither cozy nor collusive (Swaffield 2007). Bloom et al. argued that "critical" is the highest level of thought (as cited in Andreu et al., 2003, p. 35), and Senge compared the concepts of "dialogue" vs. "discussion" to emphasize the importance of impartiality and being open to progress (as cited in MacBeath, 1998, p. 128). As a result, the students in the Mental Health Education cohort had become a tightly knit group more than capable of engaging in and sustaining challenging dialogue. The culture and practices of Critical Friendships, though not in name, continues to be the norm for this cohort. Given this, my goal in the MIE course was to

deeply engage the students in mindfulness practices while at once expos-
ing them to literature cautious or critical of mindfulness in the West.

A Brief Synopsis of Course Content and an Overarching Goal

The guiding questions for the course belie my hermeneutic background. Hermeneutic philosopher Hans-Georg Gadamer (1900–2002) be-
lieved we needed to understand how our history and traditions shape us,
what he termed as "historically-effected consciousness" (2004, pp.
336–37). I remind educators that where we are now in our quick and
excited take-up of the newest and best interventions in education is almost always reflected in our history, and thus there can be something of a
possible ignorance or unknowing and uncritical inheritance happening
when we find ourselves enamoured with new approaches. Dialoguing
over why we are excited by these approaches and, how our history has
informed and, in some ways generated new approaches, is important. I
suggest that the cultivation of such historical awareness allows for a discerning attention to the present moment. This is mindfulness.

For these reasons, in the courses I teach relevant and often marginalized or concealed histories are shared. In the MIE course students were
asked to read chapter two of *Teaching Mindfulness* (McCown, Reibel, and
Micozzi, 2010), titled "A History Exercise to Locate Mindfulness Now."
Given that history, students were asked to read various peer-reviewed
articles in which authors contest the current popularity of secular mindfulness in the West. At the same time, students read articles supporting
MIE, including meta-analysis of current research literature.

Thus the historical background was opened up and, the current to-
pography or map of what we could describe as "mindfulness camps" is
laid open for students to see and explore. While this was taking place, I
facilitated many mindfulness practices from *Teaching Mindfulness*
(McCown, Reibel, and Micozzi, 2010), followed by dialogue about those
experiences. Students were also given a brief introduction to mindfulness
as it resides in the Buddhist system, so they could see how the various
MIE camps do and do not embrace the larger Buddhist system and values.

On their own time students were also reading, in small groups, one
book from a selection of books on specific MIE programs for use in P–12
settings. Examples of books selected from include *Learning to BREATHE*
(Broderick, 2013), *The MindUp Curriculum* (2011), and *Mindful Teaching
and Teaching Mindfulness* (Schoeberlein and Sheth, 2009), to name a few.
Near the end of the course student groups had one hour to share their
books with the entire class, including engaging their peers in at least one
book-based mindfulness practice. At the end of the course students submitted a daily mindfulness practice journal. We were well immersed in
mindfulness practices and scholarly work.

The course was structured through the guiding questions as outlined above with the hope of meeting the goals of our graduate programs. In particular, I hoped that students would begin to think historically and critically about MIE, as well as see that facilitated mindfulness practices for adults can be helpful, but not without emotional intensity. MIE should not be taken up lightly, as an easy set of strategies for self or student practice.

For example, popular education topics come and go. However, historical awareness, alongside critical thinking and tactful, present minded awareness can help us discern if such topics are worthwhile in our present contexts. Such practical judgement does not arise solely out of training in programs that are filled with strategies for application to students. Practical judgement arises out of practice, and a reflective, noticing practice that is mindful of how much the present moment is shaped by a larger, multi-vocal, and complex history. I was attempting to develop the continued cultivation of this practical judgement in my students (and myself), which is a disposition of always seeing oneself and one's work as being in progress. This is also to not take one's experience for granted, rather to know that experience can show and teach us our limits, again and again.

Single stories (Adichie, 2009) of the power of mindfulness foreclose the possibility that those around us, including critics of secular mindfulness, might have something to teach us. We might do well to know of such concerns and, in our particular locales, heed such warnings. This attitude and knowledge seeking is, I offer, a hermeneutic or mindful one. Given this, more needs to be said about McMindfulness and what is at play for us, in MIE.

At Play: McMindfulness

In mindfulness, an ongoing dialogue is occurring between Eastern-oriented, tradition-based mindfulness instructors/scholars, and those espousing or teaching a secularized mindfulness. Their concerns with the secular uptake of mindfulness have been described as McMindfulness (Hyland, 2015a, 2015b; Purser, 2015; Purser and Loy, 2013). At its core, the main concern is with the apparent application of mindfulness to activities and practices that do not align with the core values of compassion, loving kindness, sympathetic joy (true joy for those who we believe have more than we do, or can do more than we can), and equanimity (composure), inherent to traditional mindfulness practices (McCown, Reibel, and Micozzi, 2010).

That some large corporations have embraced mindfulness has many concerned about the goals or outcomes such practices are intended to support (Hyland, 2015a, 2015b; Purser, 2015; Purser and Loy, 2013). Is mindfulness being used to increase corporate profits by helping employees make more mindful business decisions, including becoming more skilled at profit making? A starker example comes from the United States military's adoption of mindfulness training for its soldiers (Gregoire, 2015; Shonin and Van Gordon, 2014). Should mindfulness be used to cultivate better killing skills? In the secularization of mindfulness, it is claimed that the core values of the traditional practice appear forgotten or outright ignored. In the intense pursuit of the "benefits" of the often singular injunction to be in the moment, present minded, with non-judgemental awareness (Kabat-Zinn and Univ. of Mass. Medical Center, 1990), have we forgotten or chosen to ignore that the universal values in mindfulness, at least according to Buddhism, lies in an eightfold path to human enlightenment of which right mindfulness is but one of the ways?

But what does McMindfulness have to do with MIE? Some scholars in education share similar concerns to the above, especially when secular-ized MIE is often taken up with a hyper-focus on helping students con-trol themselves better, known as self-regulation or, as a skill-set that changes the brain structure so students are better learners (Mackenzie, 2015; Reveley, 2015). This focus, in itself, does not appear troubling. Through MIE educators and students can be better at getting on with education. This focus could be seen as a response to perennial concerns we have with students we see as troubled or "at risk," including those with mental health problems or illnesses, for examples. Classrooms are diverse in such ways, and the demands placed upon teachers seem to require yet another approach to making these situations better for every-one. It is no wonder MIE is taken up with such zeal. MIE books and programs, websites, and institutes, both profit and non-profit, abound. They are an answer to the troubling phenomenon that has existed at least as far back as the creation of the modern school: How do we help stu-dents in need?

Surely, the secular application of mindfulness in these regards is help-ful for both educators and students. The burgeoning data says so, as does the experience of many educators who have applied mindfulness prac-tices to their classrooms. So what is the concern with MIE? What can often get missed in a hyper-focus on the student and their inherent "dys-regulation" or disorder, is a more self-reflective focus on educator peda-gogy and the ways we enact curriculum in classrooms. An educator can teach an array of mindfulness practices and skills to students so they can "self-regulate," without any teacher reflection on, or change in teaching style. Yet, an educator's self-practice of mindful noticing can reveal taken for granted ways of teaching, as well as presumptions about how stu-dents learn. This noticing might even reveal how teaching and learning can be a part of the production of "dysregulation" in students (Gilham, 2012a; Gilham, 2012b; Gilham and Jardine, 2015). During my time as a school board consultant I was able to observe many classrooms. I often found educators overly focussed on the dysfunction they saw in students with little to no reflection on how their classroom culture and practices played a role in the generation or exacerbation of that troubling student dysfunction.

How might mindfulness—as a way of being—not be reduced to another strategy or instrument in the ongoing accumulation of interventions used on students "for their own good," so to speak? The classroom has increasingly become a therapeutic milieu (Ecclestone and Hayes, 2009), perhaps at the cost of seeing how we counter-productively contribute to the conditions that make us believe we need that milieu by consistently engaging students with curriculum in ways that produce the phenomenon and, the specific psycho-educational language of dysregulation.

Put differently yet again, how might mindfulness break open the dominance of the deficit discourse, and our hyper-focus on the individual student and her problems? How might mindfulness create critical dialogue with self and our students to create new solidarities towards rich and engaging teaching and learning? Otherwise, we could interpret the current popularity and uptake of MIE as a form of McMindfulness: cleverly packaged, stream-lined, easy to use tools to help students be docile in the face of disengaging teaching and learning environments. I am suggesting that MIE can be taken up such that it actually conceals Critical Friendships with self and others, while reinforcing the troubles with "kids these days." Curriculum theorist Dr. David Jardine, using a Tibetan Buddhist metaphor, presents this challenge for us:

> What very often happens in schools when students become restless and encounter difficulties with the work they face is that teachers (and sometimes assessors, testers, curriculum developers, and remediators) zoom in on that trouble, narrowing attention, making the "meadow," the "field of relations" available to that restless student less huge, luscious, rich and spacious (this defines, of course, precisely what can happen to a restless teacher in a school as well). As Trungpa notes, paranoia and limitation increase in response to restlessness. In a tragic but terribly understandable turn, restlessness begins to be blamed on the fact that the field is too big, too luscious, alluring and distracting. . . . Tasks facing a restless student become stupider, more menial and demeaning, more degrading to be part of, less interesting, less alluring, and all of this because of the student and their restlessness. The more trouble a student has, the smaller and simpler and less interesting the "bit" doled out to them.
>
> And the more restless they become.
>
> And the more our paranoia and need for limitedness increases.
>
> To hark back to Chogyam Trungpa's words, in the process of such narrowing,
>
> > restlessness does not become irrelevant. It becomes paramount. The restlessness now no longer has places ("fields") that are patient,

forgiving, variegated, rich and rigorous enough so that our trou-
bledness
 might be able to work itself out.
 It can now only be worked on.
 Poor restless cow has a problem.
(Personal email exchange)

Teaching becomes narrowed, and hyper-structured in order to silence the
restless, "abnormal" student. Instead, freer spaces for teaching and learning (Jardine, 2012) are needed. If one puts the restless cow in a large, rich,
open field (of inquiry based learning, for example), the restlessness becomes irrelevant: the student finds meaningful engagement in learning.
How might a mindful practice aimed towards the very work we do cultivate compassion, loving kindness, sympathetic joy, and equanimity towards teaching and learning? Compassion for students trapped in restricted, meaningless, and boring teaching and learning conditions might
be just what is called for, but most MIE discussions singularly focus on
student self-regulation and social emotional learning. It's the student's
work only, not ours. This doesn't quite seem mindful. This content was
the culminating, final dialogue of the MIE course.

As Research

Given the above, and as the focus of a research project, I asked, "What
are the impacts of this course on the educators who took it, both during
and two months after and, by extension, what do those impacts have to
say about MIE and in-service teacher education?" Students who completed the course had two options for participating, if they choose to
participate: they could consent to let me use their course work for this
research, or they could consent to my use of their course work and answer the following guiding questions:

1. Since our summer course together, describe how mindfulness does
   or does not play a role in how you perceive and act within your
   school/classroom or personal life.
2. If mindfulness has played a role in your school/classroom life, was
   this direct or indirect, or both? In other words, did you talk specifically about mindfulness with peers or students or were you indirectly being mindful in your daily work/life? Try to provide an
   anecdote.
3. Describe any felt or lived challenges to being mindful in schools/
   classrooms.
4. Did our critical analysis of mindfulness in education play a role in
   seeing or understanding these challenges? If yes, how so?

5. Has being part of a close-knit cohort (critical friendships) played a role in your understanding and experience of mindfulness? If yes, how so?
6. Describe how you might use mindfulness in education in your future work.

Of the 18 students in the course, 10 submitted consents for use of their course-based work. Of those 10 participants, 7 answered the post-course reflection questions. Consent forms were sent directly to me. Post-course writing responses were sent to a faculty member who removed all identification from the responses. In the remainder of this chapter I will share themes that emerged from the participant post-course responses.

Themes and the Cultivation of Practical Judgement

Five themes emerged from the data. The first theme aligns with current literature on MIE and mental health. The next three themes align with the values inherent to traditional mindfulness. I did not expect to see or make this connection in this research however, my bias in connecting these themes together is also a strength, I would offer, particularly since I have attempted to reveal and reinforce the need to avoid MIE as simply a self-regulating tool, another form of McMindfulness. The fifth theme of cultivating conditions for teachers to engage with one another in particular professional contexts connects to and, perhaps synthesizes the four others. All of these themes work together I suggest, towards the cultivation of practical judgement, a form of character presented in Aristotle's (384 BC–322 BC) work (translation by Ross and Urmson, 1980) and taken up in earnest in Gadamer's Hermeneutics (2004).

1. This first theme was universal and predominant. I describe it as *Increased Educator Mental Health*, resonant with current literature on MIE and teacher education (Benn et al., 2012; Beshai et al., 2015; Flook et al., 2013; Gold et al., 2010; Jennings et al., 2011; Jennings et al., 2013; Mañas, Franco and Justo, 2011; Meiklejohn et al., 2012; Metis Associates, 2011; Napoli, 2004; Roeser et al., 2013; Taylor et al., 2015). Two months after the course, participants shared feeling an increased sense of calmness, an awareness of one's emotional states, reduced stress, less rumination on tasks yet to do, and, increased acceptance of where they were at in life and work, for examples.

Important to this discussion, three other themes emerged that have strong resonances with key values in Buddhist thought (McCown, Reibel, and Micozzi, 2010). These themes are:

2. The Importance of Critical Friendships that students had established with one another in the cohort, prior to taking the course. This resonates especially closely with Compassion and Equanimity.

- The cohort ". . . allowed me to open myself up to the experience. I was not guarded, like I might be with a group that I didn't know so well . . . I felt accountable to the others, like we were all on this journey together, so I was deeply committed to my mindfulness practice during that time . . . I also worked my active listening muscles and grew in my empathy for others."
- "By being comfortable with my peers I was able to share things that I would not normally share with close friends and family."
- ". . . it (their relationships) allowed us to practice in a secure atmosphere, it gives me a network of support that I can call on anytime . . . I cannot express my gratitude for having been placed in the base group with (name of two peers in the cohort), their patience, creativity and gentleness have allowed me to explore more of the mindful side of the program."
- Another participant wrote of first feeling "self-conscious and judgemental about my own experience" but "since I was a part of close-knit cohort, I felt like it was okay to share these feelings of doubt without fear or judgment . . . as we practiced mindfulness heavy emotions quickly bubbled to the surface. The floodgate of tears was constantly open and represented fear, joy, panic and many other mixed emotions. I felt safe letting these emotions out . . . and only felt compassion and support from my classmates. . . . If I had done this course with a group of people I did not know, I would have stifled these feelings."
- Another participant shared feeling "safe to try and experience new things as you know you are not being judged or ridiculed for trying something new. I felt the discussions during the course were insightful, thought-provoking and challenged the status quo" and they were led "by the cohort."
- "The level of trust and camaraderie that we have built in this cohort allowed me to be honest in my opinion/interpretation of mindfulness as a tool for self-exploration and examination of the world around me. The candid insights and criticism from the group and the instructor made me feel I was not alone in my interpretation and that my experience was not completely out of the norm. I experienced a great deal of support from the group as a whole as well as from individuals within the group."

3. *Composure in the Face of Stressful Work Lives* resonant with the value of *equanimity*.

- ". . . schools can be time-starved, data-focused, stress hubs . . . it is my opinion that schools are, increasingly, places of stress for teachers, students and administrators . . . (mindfulness supports) a growing ability to respond rather than react to situations."
- "In a busy world of teaching where there are lots of classes, conflicts, misunderstandings among colleagues over a whole host of things "XXXX Book" has allowed me to separate my visceral emotions from getting caught up in things that will lead to non-productive outcomes."
- Mindfulness helped ". . . the creation of a space that allows us to *choose* how we respond to situations, as opposed to just mindlessly reacting in habitual ways . . . to put things in perspective and to let go of things that are not as pressing as I led myself to believe."
- Another participant wanted to ". . . continue reminding myself to be mindful, especially in moments of stress."
- ". . . I also become mindful, before I am going to make a difficult parent phone call or have a difficult conversation with staff or students, or parents" noting that ". . . everyday can be a challenge as we often get sucked into the what ifs or should have beens or we lose perspective of the moment and get wrapped up in a power struggle with others or ourselves."
- "I am better able to help others, my children and students, to work through some of their feelings of anger, just by helping them understand that it's important to feel their feelings but not to allow them to take over their lives—to more readily/easily let go. I'm improving in this area myself as well . . . one day at a time!"
- "I . . . use the practice indirectly, primarily for myself, taking deep breaths and remembering to slow things down. "

4. *Openness or Vulnerability* resonant with the values of *Loving Kindness, Compassion, and Sympathetic Joy.*

- "The course allowed me to understand that it's OK to fail and to learn from the failure and continue on . . . "
- Another participant wrote about feeling ". . . much more willing and open to trying different opportunities."
- The course has ". . . allowed me to be more confident in opening up dialogue and discussion with my teaching colleagues."
- "Hearing other people's stories and struggles was a good reminder that we are all facing our own battles."
- "The greatest challenge I perceive is allowing myself to feel the feelings I have in the moment and to "react" to them in a manner that is suitable for the situation I find myself in."
- "I am also more at ease when I am asked to do something that takes me out of my comfort zone."

Practical Judgement and a Theme for Us All

All seven post-course participants and approximately half of the student journaling from the course commented on various cautions for MIE, evidence that a cautious awareness towards popular educational interventions is present. A certain discerning disposition congruent with the purposes of graduate, scholarly study, mindfulness, and critical friendships emerged, I suggest. Two participants felt that MIE could not be mandated across a school community because mindfulness is an intensely personal journey. Another participant shared an anecdote from a class where students exposed to mindfulness began to share very sensitive personal content with the class, and there was concern about what was being opened up publicly, and how best to handle such situations. Two participants echoed this caution, noting that knowing one's students was crucial before engaging in MIE. Three participants realized the importance of establishing one's own mindfulness practices first, consistent with mindfulness literature (McCown, Reibel, and Micozzi, 2010; Shonin and Van Gordon, 2015).

I suggest that, in each of these cautions lie the roots of practical judgement: each caution is particular, and makes either implicit or explicit reference to examples, cases, or lived situations that require attention to their uniqueness. None of the participants shared generalized, glowing recommendations or condemnation for the universal application of MIE. Although no participants specifically wrote about MIE in the context of pedagogy, or teaching and learning, several did talk about the importance of building safe and caring connections with their students, and being open to dialogue.

In conclusion, the fifth theme (5) emerged, that I did not expect yet at the same time I am not surprised with: Teachers feel "better" and, feel they can do "better" when they can spend carefully planned time among trustworthy colleagues to intentionally practice mindfulness and dialogue over issues they are facing, personally and professionally. Hence, we are called forth to create such school cultures and teacher education programs. A discerning yet open mindfulness-one and other similar ways of being together can help cultivate and nurture communities where critical friendships play an important role in teacher thriving and, teaching and learning on behalf of students.

NOTES

1. The writing and research for this chapter was supported through the St.FX University Council for Research.
2. Thanks to M Ed student Anne Daniel for her work supporting this chapter.

REFERENCES

Adichie, C. (2009). The danger of a single story. TEDGlobal 2009. Retrieved from https://www.ted.com/talks/chimamanda_adichie_the_danger_of_a_single_story? language=en

Andreu, R., Canós, L., de Juana, S., Manresa, E., Rienda, L., and Tarí, J. J. (2003). Critical friends: A tool for quality improvement in universities. *Quality Assurance in Education, 11*(1), 31–36.

Aristotle,. Ross, W., and Urmson, J. (1980). *The Nicomachean ethics.* Oxford: Oxford University Press.

Bambino, D. (2002). Critical friends. *Educational Leadership, 59*(6), 25–27.

Benn, R., Akiva, T., Arel, S., and Roeser, R. W. (2012). Mindfulness training effects for parents and educators of children with special needs. *Developmental Psychology, 48*(5), 1476–87.

Beshai, S., McAlpine, L., Weare, K. and Kuyken, W. (2015). A non-randomized feasibility trial assessing the efficacy of a mindfulness based intervention for teachers to reduce stress and improve well-being. *Mindfulness.* Springer US, 1–11. doi: 10.1007/s12671-015-0436-1

Burke, C. A. (2010). Mindfulness-based approaches with children and adolescents: A preliminary review of current research in an emergent field. *Journal of Child and Family Studies, 19,* 133–44.

Butler, H. (2011). *The Critical Friend.* Victoria, Australia: Acer Press.

Broderick, P. C. (2013). *Learning to breathe: A mindfulness curriculum for adolescents to cultivate emotion regulation, attention, and performance.* Oakland, CA: New Harbinger.

Costa, A. L., and Kallick, B. (1993). Through the lens of a critical friend. *Educational Leadership* 51: 49–51.

Ecclestone, K., and Hayes, D. (2009). *The dangerous rise of therapeutic education.* London: Routledge.

Ergas, O. (2014) Mindfulness in education at the intersection of science, religion, and healing. *Critical Studies in Education, 55*(1), 58–72

Flook, L., Goldberg, S. B., Pinger, L., Bonus, K., and Davidson, R. J. (2013). Mindfulness for teachers: a pilot study to assess effects on stress, burnout, and teaching efficacy. *Mind, Brain, and Education, 7,* 182–95.

Gadamer, H-G. (2004). *Truth and method.* London: Continu

Gilham, C. (2012a). From the "science of disease" to the "understanding of those who suffer": The cultivation of an interpretive understanding of "behaviour problems" in children. *Journal of Applied Hermeneutics,* http://jah.synergiesprairies.ca/jah/index. php/jah/article/view/33/pdf

Gilham, C. (2012b). The privileges chart in a behaviour class: Seeing the power and complexity of dominant traditions and unconcealing trust as basic to pedagogical relationships." *Journal of Applied Hermeneutics.* http://jah.synergiesprairies.ca/jah/ index.php/jah/article/view/15/pdf

Gilham, C and Jardine, D. (2014–2015). "Cultivating the possible in the understanding of human suffering: A brief on alternatives." Canadian Association of Educational Psychologists, *Dialogic.*

Gold, E., Smith, A., Hopper, I., Herne, D., Tansey, G., and Hulland C. (2010) Mindfulness-Based Stress Reduction for primary school teachers. *Journal of Child and Family Studies* 19, no. 2: 184–89.

Gregoire, C. (2015, February 18). Mindfulness training improves resilience of active-duty soldiers. *The Huffington Post.* Retrieved from http://www.huffingtonpost.com/ 2015 /02/18/ mindfulness-military-_n_6704804.html

Huppert, F. A., and Johnson, D. A. (2010). A controlled trial of mindfulness training in schools: The importance of practice for an impact on well-being. *Journal of Positive Psychology, 5,* 264–74. doi:10.1080/17439761003794148

Hyland, T. (2015a, May 20). On the contemporary applications of mindfulness: Some implications for education. *Journal of Philosophy and Education, 49*(2), 170–86.

Hyland, T. (2015b, May 13). McMindfulness in the workplace: Vocational learning and the commodification of the present moment. *Journal of Vocational Education and Training, 67*(2), 219–34, doi: 10.1080/13636820.2015.1022871

Jardine, D. W. (2012). *Pedagogy left in peace: Cultivating free spaces in teaching and learning*. London: Continuum.

Jennings, P. A., Snowberg, K. E., Coccia, M., and Greenberg, M. T. (2011). Improving classroom learning environments by cultivating awareness and resilience in education (CARE): Results of two pilot studies. *Journal of Classroom Interaction* 46, no. 1: 37–48.

Jennings, P., Lantieri, L., and Roeser, R. W. (2012). Supporting educational goals through cultivating mindfulness: Approaches for teachers and students. In P. M. Brown, M. W. Corrigan, and A. Higgins-D'Alessandro (Eds.), *Handbook of prosocial education*. Lanham, MD: Rowman and Littlefield.

Jennings, P. A., Frank, J. L., Snowberg, K. E., Coccia, M. A., and Greenberg, M. T. (2013). Improving classroom learning environments by Cultivating Awareness and Resilience in Education (CARE): Results of a randomized controlled trial. *School Psychology Quarterly* 28, no. 4: 374–90.

Kabat-Zinn, J., and University of Massachusetts Medical Center/Worcester. (1990). *Full catastrophe living: Using the wisdom of your body and mind to face stress, pain, and illness*. New York: Delacorte Press.

MacBeath, J. (1998). I didn't know he was ill: The role and value of the critical friend. In K. Myers and L. Stoll (Eds.), *No quick fixes: Perspectives on schools in difficulty* (pp. 118–33). London: Falmer Press.

MacKenzie, E. (2015). Mindfulness Training: A transdiciplinary approach to assessing efficacy in education. In Ragoonaden, K. (2015). *Mindful teaching and learning: Developing a pedagogy of well-being*. Lanham, MD: Lexington.

Mañas, I., Franco, C., and Justo, E. M. (2011). Reducing levels of teacher stress and days of sick leave in secondary school teachers through a mindfulness training programme. *Clínica y Salud, 22*(2), 121–37.

McCown, D., Reibel, D., and Micozzi, M. S. (2010). *Teaching mindfulness: A practical guide for clinicians and educators*. New York: Springer.

McDonald, E. and Shirley, D. (2009). *The mindful teacher*. New York: Teachers College Press.

Meiklejohn, J., Phillips, C., Freedman, M. L., Griffin, M., Biegel, G., Roach, A., Frank, J., Burke, C., Pinger, L., Soloway, G., Isberg, R., Sibinga, E., Grossman, L., Saltzman, A., (2012). Integrating mindfulness training into K–12 education: Fostering the resilience of teachers and students. *Mindfulness, 3*(4), 291–307.

Metis Associates. (2011). Building inner resilience in teachers and their students: Results of the inner resilience pilot program. Retrieved November 27, 2015 from the Inner Resilience Program web site: http://innerresilience.org/documents/ IRP _Pilot_Program_Results_AERA2011_updated_6.9.pdf.

Napoli, M. (2004). Mindfulness training for teachers: A pilot program. *Complementary Health Practice Review, 9*(1), 31–42. doi:10.1177/1076167503253435.

Olsen, K. (2014). *The invisible classroom: Relationships, neuroscience and mindfulness in school*. New York: W. W. Norton and Company.

Purser, R. and Loy, D. (2013, July 1). Beyond mcmindfulness. The Huffington Post. Retrieved from: http://www.huffingtonpost.com/ron-purser/beyond-mcmindful ness_b_3519289.html

Purser, R. E. (2015). Clearing the Muddled Path of Traditional and Contemporary Mindfulness: A Response to Monteiro, Musten, and Compson. *Mindfulness* 6, no. 1: 23–45.

Ragoonaden, K., (Ed.). (2015). *Mindful teaching and learning: Developing a pedagogy of well-being*. Lanham, MD: Lexington.

Reveley, J. (2015). School-based mindfulness training and the economisation of attention: A Stieglerian view. *Educational Philosophy and Theory*. Advance online publication. doi:10.1080/00131857.2014.914880.

Roeser, R., Skinner, E., Beers, J. and Jennings, P. (2012). Mindfulness training and teachers' professional development: An emerging area of research and practice. *Child Development Perspectives, 6*(2), 167–73.

Roeser, R., Schonert-Reichl, K., Jha, A., Cullen, M., Wallace, L., Wilensky, R., Oberle, E., Thomson, K., Taylor, C., Harrison, J., Graesser, A. (editor). (2013). Mindfulness training and reductions in teacher stress and burnout: Results from two random-ized, waitlist-control field trials. *Journal of Educational Psychology, 105*(3), 787–804.

Rotne, N. and Rotne, D. (2013). *Everybody present: Mindfulness in education.* Berkeley, CA: Parallax Press.

Schoeberlein, D., and Sheth, S. (2009) *Mindful Teaching and Teaching Mindfulness: A Guide for Anyone Who Teaches Anything.* Somerville, MA: Wisdom Publications.

Shonin, E., and Van Gordon, W. (2014). Should mindfulness be taught to the military? Retrieved August 8 from http://edoshonin.com/2014/08/08/should-mindfulness-be-taught-to-the-military/

Shonin, E., and Van Gordon, W. (2015). Practical Recommendations for Teaching Mindfulness Effectively. *Mindfulness* 6, no. 4: pp. 952–55 .

Skinner, E.A., and Beers, J.C. Mindfulness and teachers' coping in the classroom: A developmental model of teacher stress, coping, and everyday resilience. Retrieved from https://www.pdx.edu/psy/sites/www.pdx.edu.psy/files/HME%20Skinner%20%26%20Beers%2022Sept2014.pdf

Storey, V. (2013). *Redesigning professional education doctorates: Applications of Critical Friendship Theory to the EdD.* New York: Palgrave Macmillan

Swaffield, S. (2002, January). *Contextualizing the work of the critical friend.* Paper present-ed at the 15th International Congress for School Effectiveness and Improvement (ICSEI), Copenhagen, January 3–6

Swaffield, S. (2003, October). Critical friendship. *[Inform No. 3] Leadership for learning.* Cambridge: University of Cambridge Faculty of Education. Retrieved from https://www.educ.cam.ac.uk/centres/lfl/about /inform/PDFs/InForm_3.pdf

Swaffield, S. (2004). Critical friends: Supporting leadership, improved learning. *Im-proving Schools* 7, no. 3: 267–78.

Swaffield, S. (2007). Light touch critical friendship. *Improving Schools* 10, no. 3: 205–19.

Swaffield, S. (2008). Critical friendship, dialogue and learning, in the context of leader-ship for learning. *School Leadership and Management* 28, no. 4: 323–36. doi: 10.1080/13632430802292191.

Taylor, C., Harrison, J., Haimovitz, K., Oberle, E., Thomson, K., Schonert-Reichl, K., Roeser R. (2015). Examining ways that a mindfulness-based intervention reduces stress in public school teachers: A mixed-methods study. *Mindfulness.* Springer US, 1–15. doi:10.1007/s12671-015-0425-4.

The MindUp curriculum: Brain-focused strategies for learning-and living. (2011). New York: Scholastic.

EIGHT

Kindness

A Mindful Act of Well-Being

John-Tyler Binfet

An examination of current evidence-based trends in education reveal a number of fields that support students' social and emotional well-being. These fields respond to a collective recognition by varied educational and workplace stakeholders of the importance of focusing on the development of the entire individual, not uniquely his or her academic abilities or workplace technical proficiencies. This is perhaps most evident in the marked changes seen in the emotional landscape of classrooms where there has been a surge of interest in initiatives that address what has been referred to at the K–12 level as social and emotional learning (SEL) (Durlak, Domitrovich, Weissberg, and Gullotta, 2015; Durlak, Weissberg, Dymnicki, Taylor, and Schellinger, 2011) and within post-secondary and work force contexts as "soft skills"—skills that include communication and interpersonal abilities and the ability to cooperate and work collaboratively, demonstrate integrity, and cultivate a positive disposition or outlook (Heckman and Kautz, 2012; Robles, 2012).

This recent emphasis on the social and emotional competencies of learners is in stark contrast to what has historically been the primary focus of many schools—academic achievement (Cohen, 2006; Schonert-Reichl and Hymel, 2007). It was largely argued and feared in many educational contexts that any emphasis on soft skills (also referred to as "non-cognitive skills") in the classroom came at the expense of achievement in core academics or "hard skills." This increased receptivity by educators to initiatives that bolster students' social and emotional skills was grounded in the recognition that students are arriving to school increasingly underequipped to meet the social and emotional demands both expected and needed within the school context (Eccles and Roeser, 2011; Jones and Bouffard, 2012; Rimm-Kaufman, Pianta, and Cox, 2000; Spivak and Farran, 2012). For some students, especially those living in fast-paced environments with little parental support or community engagement, teachers can often be the primary mechanism, and classrooms the primary context, through which students are socially and emotionally prepared for life's challenges (Downey, 2008).

Concerns over how well students are socially and emotionally prepared for school-related challenges are not restricted to the K–12 grades. Increasingly, concerns have been voiced over the ability of university students to manage stress and workload demands characteristic of postsecondary education (Heck et al., 2014). The social and emotional competencies of university students, most notably around their ability to manage stress and maintain optimal mental health, have been identified as areas in which students are lacking and require additional support (Bitsika, Sharpley, and Rubenstein, 2010; Hindman, Glass, Arnkoff, and Maron, 2015). Progressive post-secondary administrators are increasingly recognizing the importance of concurrently supporting students' academic growth and achievement as well as their social and emotional well-being. Traditional academic support systems such as writing and tutoring centers have long been in place and formal health-related resources are typically available through Student Health Services offices, but more than ever, universities are including informal opportunities for students to reduce their stress while on campus, recognizing that elevated levels of stress have implications for students' physical and psychological health (Hindman, Glass, Arnkoff, and Maron, 2015; Schneiderman, Ironson, and Seigel, 2005). As an illustration of the support offered to combat stress in university students and a reflection of a popular trend across many North American campuses, an innovative program titled "B.A.R.K." ("Building Academic Retention through K9s") at the University of British Columbia, Okanagan provides stressed and homesick students opportunities to proactively reduce their stress throughout the school year by interacting with therapy dogs. Interventions assessing pre- to post-test changes arising from exposure to therapy dogs indicate significant positive effects on students' well-being with reductions in stress and homesickness and increases in students' campus affinity evident (Binfet and Passmore, in press).

Understanding Social and Emotional Learning

The development of students' social and emotional competencies is most explicitly addressed by the field of SEL, a field supported by researchers and practitioners in both education (e.g., Elias, Zins, Weissberg,

Frey, Greenberg, Haynes, et al., 1997; Jennings, 2011; Schonert-Reichl, Hanson-Peterson, and Hymel, 2015) and psychology (e.g., Blair and Raver, 2015; Greenberg, Katz, and Cousino-Klein, 2015). In a recent handbook on SEL by Durlak, Domitrovich, Weissberg, and Gullotta (2015), SEL is defined as: "implementing practices and policies that help children and adults acquire and apply the knowledge, skills, and attitudes that can enhance personal development, establish satisfying relationships, and lead to effective and ethical work and productivity" (Weissberg, Durlak, Domitrovich, and Gulotta, 2015, p. 6).

Over time, initiatives grounded in SEL have flourished. There is now a plethora of programs available for younger students, though there is a relative dearth of programs targeted to students at the secondary and post-secondary levels (Williamson, Modecki, and Guerra, 2015). At the core of many programs are the five pillars of SEL identified by the Collaborative for Academic and Social and Emotional Learning (CASEL, 2013): self-awareness, self-management, social awareness, relationship skills, and responsible decision-making. Many of the SEL programs available to educators are developed around these five pillars, though thematic variations have emerged (e.g., the Heart-Mind Index from the Dalai Lama Centre for Peace and Education uses the following pillars: "Gets along with others," "Alert and engaged," "Compassionate and kind," "Solves problems peacefully," and "Secure and calm"). Coinciding with the surge in popularity of SEL, has been the identification of challenges arising around educator training and around how programs have been administered or what is referred to in program evaluation as "implementation fidelity"—the extent to which programs are delivered as intended—with the proper a priori training, protocols, and dosage (for a review of factors impacting the efficacy of SEL program delivery see Durlak, 2015).

A seminal article, published in *Child Development* by Joseph Durlak and colleagues (2011), served to propel interest in SEL. Now cited over 1,500 times in subsequent academic publications, their meta-analytic review of 213 SEL interventions (surveying a collective sample of over 270,000 participants) revealed not only benefits to students' social and emotional development but a resultant increase in students' academic scores (upwards of 11 to 17 percentile points). Across studies, students who participated in school-based SEL programs, "demonstrated enhanced SEL skills, attitudes, and positive social behaviors following the intervention and also demonstrated fewer conduct problems and had lower levels of emotional distress" when compared to counterparts in control conditions (Durlak et al., 2011, p. 9). The importance of these findings are not to be understated, as they gave permission for educators, who intuitively knew the importance of promoting SEL but may have been wary to stray from a "traditional academic" focus, to teach in ways they knew to be beneficial for students. This was the green light that many educators had been awaiting as it showed that incorporating SEL benefitted not only students' social and emotional competencies but also their academic achievement.

Though it was the identification of the value added, the gain in academic scores, that helped pave the way for SEL in classrooms and schools, in contrast, it was the lack of SEL among employees that heralded the need for SEL in the workplace, and subsequently in post-secondary education (James and James, 2005; Klaus, 2010; Nealy, 2005; Robles, 2012). Colleges and universities are the staging ground where students are not only educated in their disciplines, but are prepared for the challenges of the workplace. Employees who are able to navigate the social and emotional challenges of the workplace are more productive than those who stumble over these challenges, resulting in lower professional attrition and costly employee turnover. As the purpose of education is often touted as the preparation of students for membership in, and contribution to, society, particularly the labor force, it is perhaps not surprising that a shared recognition for the importance of social and emotional competencies has been found concomitantly in the classroom and the boardroom. Though estimates vary, different authors have proffered that hard skills account only for 15–25 percent of long-term job success with soft skills accounting for the bulk of stable workplace employment (John, 2009; Klaus, 2010). This recognition for the need for SEL arose from workers with ample hard skills (i.e., technical expertise) struggling to maintain employment and the realization that their challenges were anchored in a deficit in social and emotional competencies required for optimal functioning in the workplace.

In response to the social and emotional competencies lacking across varied contexts, a number of fields of study have found traction. The surge in interest in SEL is paralleled by increased interest in other fields whose broad aims are to promote well-being, including, Positive Psychology (Seligman and Csikszentimihalyi, 2000), Positive Education (Seligman, Earnst, Gillham, Reivich, and Linkins, 2009) and Mindfulness (Frank, Jennings, and Greenberg, 2013; Kabat-Zinn, 1994). Mindfulness is of particular importance for the current discussion as it lays the foundation for "other-oriented dispositions" including empathy, compassion, altruism, forgiveness, generosity, and most importantly for this chapter, the enacting of kindness (Roeser and Pinela, 2014).

Mindfulness as a Foundation for Kindness

There are a number of features or properties of mindfulness that can be drawn upon to support the enacting of intentional kindness. "Mindfulness interventions primarily target self-awareness and self-management skills, with some focus also on social awareness and relationship skills, by training the mind to function in a mode of moment-to-moment awareness, acceptance, nonjudgment, and compassion" (Conley, 2015, p. 200). There are multiple benefits to practicing mindfulness, ranging from the reduction of anxiety (Miller, Fletcher, and Kabat-Zinn, 1995) to the strengthening of social skills (Beauchemin, Hutchins, and Patterson, 2008). The awareness of self and of others arising from practicing mindfulness can prove useful in encouraging individuals, especially young students, to behave prosocially through what has been coined *Intentional Acts of Kindness* (IAK) (Binfet, 2015). The notion of performing "random acts of kindness" has become fairly pervasive in Western culture but it is argued here that both structure and intentionality (thus the opposite of behaving randomly) are needed to support students in their cultivation of kind behavior and habits. Moreover, it can be argued that the encouragement of IAK may very well lead to the creation of habits and dispositions that encourage random acts of kindness.

Enacting IAK requires reflection that may be supported by mindfulness. For example, encouraging students to reflect in the following three steps of enacting IAK can be supported by a mindfulness practice: 1) identifying possible recipients (i.e., the creation of a recipient bank), which requires perspective-taking to help students recognize familiar and unfamiliar others in their communities in need of receiving kindness; 2) identifying the gratitude of recipients (i.e., how grateful were the recipients of each act of students' kindness?), which requires perspective-taking or "other-regarding"; and 3) reflecting on the impact on students themselves arising from their being intentionally kind (e.g., how did being kind make students feel?), which requires introspection. In encouraging IAK, mindfulness may be seen as a complimentary precursor practice that lays the foundation and prepares the individual to reflect upon and consider others within his or her purview who might profit from being the recipient of intentional kindness.

There is ample support for the encouragement of kindness with parents and educators routinely encouraging students to "be kind." In fact, fostering prosocial behavior such as kindness in students is a common tenet of most schools' mission or vision statements. The BC Ministry of Education, for example, maintains that teachers are to encourage socially responsible behavior in students that includes developing skills and dispositions that enhance and enrich the classroom and school community. More specifically, the Ministry expects students to be "welcoming, friendly, kind, and helpful" (BC Ministry of Education, 2015). There is thus a declared emphasis by varied educational stakeholders that encouraging students to be kind is important. This is further reflected in research (e.g., Karris and Craighead, 2012; Park, Peterson, and Seligman, 2004) identifying that, even more than honesty, gratitude, or hope, the trait of kindness is indicated as one of the top-ranking character strengths valued in Western Society. This is also echoed in research that asks parents what they wish for their children and sees "being good" or "being kind" consistently indicated as a top desired trait (Diener and Lucas, 2004; Seligman, Ernst, Gillham, Reivich, and Linkins, 2009; Wang and Tamis-LeMonda, 2003).

Researchers wanting to know the effects of prosocial behavior such as kindness have asked participants to perform a variety of kind acts to assess their impact on well-being (Layous et al., 2012; Okake et al., 2006). These researchers have examined the dosage (how many kind acts must individuals do to reap benefits?) (Kerr, O'Donovan, and Pepping, 2014), the scheduling or timing of kind acts (Lyubomirsky, Sheldon, and Schkade, 2005), and whether doing the same or varied kind acts (Sheldon et al., 2012) is important. The study of kindness is theoretically grounded in SEL and both in positive psychology and its derivative field of positive education. What is not immediately evident in a review of the extant educational and psychological literature is the theoretical or applied links uniting mindfulness and kindness. SEL provides a theoretical framework for a discussion of kindness and mindfulness as these concepts are situated within several, if not all, of the cognitive, affective, and behavioral competencies comprising SEL (i.e., relationship skills, social awareness, self-management, self-awareness, and responsible decision-making; CASEL, 2015). Positive psychology and positive education in particular (Clonan et al., 2004; Seligman and Csikszentmihalyi, 2000; Seligman et al., 2009) also theoretically support this discussion as educators shift from viewing student behavior from a model based on "What's wrong and needs fixing?" to "What are the strengths and positive attributes of the learners I teach?" Encouraging a mindfulness practice and IAK within school contexts are initiatives in alignment with the overarching themes of supporting students' well-being.

Educational Trends Supporting Mindfulness and Kindness

As educators strive to encourage mindfulness and kindness in students as a means of promoting healthy development, two exciting educational transitions are taking place. Firstly, educators are increasingly fostering students' social and emotional growth not in distinct silos, separate and alongside academic subject matter, but through instruction embedded within the promotion of core academic content (Elias et al., 2015; Flook, Goldberg, Pinger, and Davdison, 2015; Schonert-Reichl, Hanson-Peterson, and Hymel, 2015). In response to the recognized benefits of enriching core academic content with social and emotional content, lessons are transforming to accommodate the inclusion of SEL.

A second transition that is underway in schools challenges the emphasis historically placed upon preventing or managing unkind and antisocial acts, such as bullying. New initiatives are in motion emphasizing the prosocial behavior desired from students rather than the behavior students are to avoid. Support for this shift is derived from findings indicating that "Despite all the attention paid to reducing bullying, meta-analytic findings by Smith and colleagues (Smith, Schneider, Smith, and Ananiadou, 2004) and as argued by others (e.g., Pryce and Fredrickson, 2013), whole-school anti-bullying programs have not resulted in significant reductions of self-reports of bullying and victimization" (Binfet and Gaertner, 2015, p. 27). Educators are increasingly embracing positive education and programs that contribute to fostering the qualities in children that contribute to successful functioning in school and turning away from investing in resources the focus of which are on identifying and highlighting undesirable school-related behaviors.

The Benefits of Being Mindful or Intentionally Kind

The recent emphasis on, and surge of interest in, school kindness is fueled, in part, by the benefits to well-being arising from being kind. Positive psychology interventions asking participants to enact kindness have resulted in a number of favorable outcomes. "Acts of kindness can build trust and acceptance between people, encourage social bonds, provide givers and receivers with the benefits of positive social interaction, and enable helpers to use and develop personal skills and thus themselves" (Kerr, O'Donovan, and Pepping, 2014, p. 20). These findings parallel or compliment many of the benefits known to arise from practicing mindfulness. Though the body of literature attesting to the benefits of mindfulness is more robust in adult populations, the study of mindfulness in children and adolescents is nevertheless an emerging area, garnering the interest of researchers and practitioners (Greenberg and Harris, 2011; Meiklejohn et al., 2012). As noted earlier, the benefits of mindfulness are varied and can include an increase in attention skills (Napoli, Krech, and Holley, 2005; Zylowska, et al., 2008), social skills (Beauchemin et al., 2008), and well-being (Huppert and Johnson, 2010).

There are a number of reasons educators might consider embracing initiatives that see both mindfulness and *Intentional Acts of Kindness* (IAK) encouraged within their classrooms and school communities. Firstly, the incorporation of these initiatives stands to benefit both the teacher him or herself and the broader educational community, notably the school climate. The focus on well-being in schools is not uniquely restricted to the promotion of well-being in students. Researchers have shed light on the benefits to teachers and school communities from encouraging practices, such as mindfulness, that help safeguard teacher well-being and prevent teacher burnout (Jennings and Greenberg, 2009). Secondly, the incorporation of initiatives grounded in mindfulness and kindness are not cost-prohibitive and need not be supported by the purchasing of expensive, pre-packaged materials. Thirdly, both the practice of mindfulness and the encouragement of IAK can be adapted to individual developmental levels. These are thus initiatives that can be embraced by all learners, within their respective developmental capabilities. Finally, encouraging students to practice mindfulness and IAK, helps build skills that will serve them both in their immediate school environment and within their future workplace contexts.

Conclusion

The themes evident within, the skills cultivated through the practice of, and the benefits arising from mindfulness and *Intentional Acts of Kindness* (IAK) foregrounded in sustainable professional development can help foster both introspective reflection and other-regarding. These skills arising through the practice of mindfulness and IAK help fortify educators in their weathering of the social and emotional challenges they will invariably face and in their ability to emerge as colleagues, community members and citizens who manage their stress and well-being and positively contribute to society at large.

REFERENCES

Beauchemin, J., Hutchins, T. L., and Patterson, F. (2008). Mindfulness may lesson anxiety, promote social skills and improve academic performance among adolescents with learning disabilities. *Complementary Health Practice Review* 13: 34–45.

Binfet, J. T. (2015). Not-so random acts of kindness: A guide to intentional kindness in the classroom. *The International Journal of Emotional Education* 7: 35–51.

Binfet, J. T., and Gaertner, A. (2015). Children's conceptualizations of kindness at school. *Canadian Children, 40,* 27–39.

Binfet, J. T., and Passmore, H. A., (in press). Hounds and homesickness: The effects of an animal-assisted therapeutic intervention for first-year university students. *Anthrozoos.*

Bitsika, V., Sharpley, C. F., and Rubenstein, V. (2010). What stresses university students: An interview investigation of the demands of tertiary studies. *Australian Journal of Guidance & Counselling* 20: 41–54.

Blair, C., and Raver, C. C. (2015). The neuroscience of SEL. In R. Weissberg, C. Domitrovich, J. Durlak, and T. Gullotta (Eds.). *The Handbook of Social and Emotional Learning (SEL): Research and Practice.* New York: Guilford Press (pp. 65–80).

British Columbia Ministry of Education (2015). Retrieved Nov. 13, 2015, from https://www.bced.gov.bc.ca/perf_stands/social_resp.htm.

Building Academic Retention through K9s (B.A.R.K.) (2015). Retrieved October 23, 2015, from http://barkubc.ca.

Clonan, S. M., Chafouleas, S. M., McDougal, J. L., and Riley-Tillman, T. C. (2004). Positive psychology goes to school: Are we there yet? *Psychology in the Schools* 41: 101–10.

Cohen, J. (2006). Social, emotional, ethical, and academic education: Creating a climate for learning, participation in democracy, and well-being. *Educational Reviewer* 76: 201–37.

Collaborative for Academic and Social and Emotional Learning (CASEL) (2013). *What is social and emotional learning (SEL)?* Retrieved September 19, 2015, from http://casel.org/why-it-matters/what-is-sel.

Conley, C. S. (2015). SEL in higher education. In R. Weissberg, C. Domitrovich, J. Durlak, and T. Gullotta (Eds.). *The Handbook of Social and Emotional Learning (SEL): Research and Practice.* New York: Guilford Press (pp. 197–212).

Diener, M. L., and Lucas, R. E. (2004). Adults' desires for children's emotions across 48 countries. *Journal of Cross-Cultural Psychology* 35: 525–47.

Downey, J. A. (2008). Recommendations for fostering educational resilience in the classroom. *Preventing School Failure* 53: 56–64.

Durlak, J. A. (2015). What everyone should know about implementation. In R. Weissberg, C. Domitrovich, J. Durlak, and T. Gullotta (Eds.). *The Handbook of Social and Emotional Learning (SEL): Research and Practice.* New York: Guilford Press (pp. 395–405).

Durlak, J. A., Domitrovich, C. E., Weissberg, R. P., and Gullotta, T. P. (2015) *Handbook of Social and Emotional Learning.* New York: The Guilford Press.

Durlak, J. A., Weissberg, R. P., Dymnicki, A.B., Taylor, R. D., and Schellinger, K. B. (2011). The impact of enhancing students' social and emotional learning: A meta-analysis of school-based interventions. *Child Development* 82: 405–32.

Eccles, J. S., and Roeser, R. W. (2011). School and community influences on human development. In M. H. Bornstein and M. E., Lamb (Eds.), *Developmental science: An advanced textbook* (6th ed., pp. 571–643). New York: Psychology Press.

Elias, M. J., Leverett, L., Cole-Duffell, J., Humphrey, N., Stepney, C., and Ferrito, J. (2015 .Integrating SEL with related prevention and youth. In R. Weissberg, C. Domitrovich, J. Durlak, and T. Gullotta (Eds.). *The Handbook of Social and Emotional Learning (SEL): Research and Practice.* New York: Guilford Press (pp. 33–49).

Elias, M. J., Zins, J. E., Weissberg, R. P., Frey, K. S., Greenberg, M. T., Haynes, N. M., et al., (1997). *Promoting social and emotional learning: Guidelines for educators.* Alexandria, VA: Association for Supervision and Curriculum Development.

Flook, L., Goldberg, S. B., Pinger, L., and Davidson, R. J. (2015). Promoting prosocial behavior and self-regulatory skills in preschool children through a mindfulness-based kindness curriculum. *Developmental Psychology, 51,* 44–51.

Frank, J. L., Jennings, P. A., and Greenberg, M. T. (2013). Mindfulness-based interventions in school settings: An introduction to the special issue. *Research in Human Development* 10: 205–10.

Greenberg, M. T., and Harris, A. R. (2011). Nurturing mindfulness in children and youth: Current state of research. *Journal of Applied School Psychology* 26: 70–95.

Greenberg, M., Katz, D., and Cousino-Klein, L. C. (2015). The potential effects of SEL on biomarkers and health outcomes. In R. Weissberg, C. Domitrovich, J. Durlak, and T. Gullotta (Eds.). *The Handbook of Social and Emotional Learning (SEL): Research and Practice.* New York: Guilford Press (pp. 81–96).

Heck, E., Jaworska, N., DeSomma, E., Dhoopa, A. S., MacMaster, F. P., Dewey, D., and MacQueen, G. (2014). A survey of mental health services at post-secondary institutions in Alberta. *Canadian Journal of Psychiatry* 59: 250–58.

Heckman, J. J., and Kautz, T. (2012). Hard evidence on soft skills. *Labour Economics* 19: 451–64.

Hindman, R. K., Glass, C. R., Arnkoff, D. B., and Maron, D. D. (2015). A comparison of formal and informal mindfulness programs for stress reduction in university students. *Mindfulness* 6: 873–84.

Huppert, F. A., and Johnson, D. M. (2010). A controlled trial of mindfulness training in schools: The importance of practice for an impact on well-being. *Journal of Positive Psychology* 5: 264–74.

James, R. F., and James, m. L. (2004). Teaching career and technical skills in a "mini" business world. *Business Education Forum, 59,* 39–41.

Jennings, P. A. (2011). Promoting teachers' social and emotional competencies to support performance and reduce burnout. In A. Cohan and A. Honigsfeld (Eds.), *Breaking the mold of preservice and inservice teacher education: Innovative and successful practices for the 21st century* (pp. 133–43). Plymouth, UK: Rowman & Littlefield Education.

Jennings, P. A., and Greenberg, M. T. (2009). The prosocial classroom: Teacher social and emotional competence in relation to student and classroom outcomes. *Review of Educational Research* 79: 491–525.

John, J. (2009, Oct./Dec.). Study on the nature of impact of soft skills training programme on the soft skills development of management students. *Pacific Business
Review*: 19–27.

Jones, S. M., and Bouffard, S. M. (2012). Social and emotional learning in schools: From
programs to strategies. *Sharing Child and Youth Development Knowledge* 26: 1–22.

Kabat-Zinn, J. (1994). *Wherever you go, there you are: Mindfulness meditation in everyday
life*. New York: Hyperion.

Karris, M. A. and Craighead, W. E. (2012). Differences in character among U.S. college
students. *Individual Differences Research* 10: 69–80.

Kerr, S. L., O'Donovan, A., and Pepping, C. A. (2014). Can gratitude and kindness
interventions enhance well-being in a clinical sample? *Journal of Happiness Studies*
16: 17–36.

Klaus, P. (2010). Communication breakdown. *California Job Journal, 28,* 1–9.

Layous, K., Nelson, K., Oberle, E., Schonert-Reichl, K., and Lyubomirsky, S. (2012).
Kindness counts: Prompting prosocial behavior in preadolescents boosts peer acceptance and well-being. *PLoS ONE* 7, no. 12: e51380. doi: 10.1371/journal
.pone.0051380

Lyubomirsky, S., Sheldon, K. M., and Schkade, D. (2005). Pursuing happiness: The
architecture of sustainable change. *Review of General Psychology* 9: 111–31.

Meiklejohn, J., Phillips, C., Freedman, M. L., Griffin, M. L., and Biegel, Roach, A. T.,
Frank, J. L. . . . Saltzman, A. (2012). Integrating mindfulness training into K–12
education: Fostering the resilience of teachers and students. *Mindfulness, 3,* 291–307.

Miller, J. J., Fletcher, K., and Kabat-Zinn, J. (1995). Three-year follow-up and clinical
implications of a mindfulness meditation-based stress reduction intervention in the
treatment of anxiety disorders. *General Hospital Psychiatry* 17: 192–200.

Napoli, M., Krech, P. R., and Holley, L. C. (2005). Mindfulness training for elementary
school students: The Attention Academy. *Journal of Applied School psychology* 21:
99–125.

Nealy, C. (2005). Integrating soft skills through active learning in the management
classroom. *Journal of College Teaching & Learning* 2: 1–6.

Otake, K., Shimai, S., Tanaka-Matsumi, J., Otsui, K., and Fredrickson, B. L. (2006).
Happy people become happier through kindness: A counting kindness intervention. *Journal of Happiness Studies* 7: 361–75. doi: 10.1007/s10902-005-3650-z

Park, N., Peterson, C. and Seligman, M.E., (2004). Strengths of character and well-
being. *Journal of Social and Clinical Psychology* 23: 603–19.

Pryce, S. and Frederickson, N. (2013). Bullying behaviour, intentions and classroom
ecology. *Learning Environment Research* 16: 183–99.

Rimm-Kaufman, S. E., Pianta, R. C., and Cox, M. J. (2000). Teachers' judgments of
problems in the transition to kindergarten. *Early Childhood Research Quarterly* 15:
147–66.

Robles, M. M. (2012). Executive perceptions of the top 10 soft skills needed in today's
workplace. *Business Communications Quarterly* 75: 453–65.

Roeser, R. W. and Pinela, C. (2014). Mindfulness and compassion training in adolescence: A developmental contemplative science perspective. *New Directions for Youth
Development* 2014: 9–30.

Schneiderman, N., Ironson, G., and Siegel, S. D. (2005). Stress and health: Psychological, behavioral, and biological determinants. *Annual Review of Clinical Psychology* 1:
607–28.

Schonert-Reichl, K. A., Hanson-Peterson, J. L., and Hymel, S. (2015). SEL and preser-
vice teacher education. In R. Weissberg, C. Domitrovich, J. Durlak, and T. Gullotta
(Eds.). *The Handbook of Social and Emotional Learning (SEL): Research and Practice.*
New York: Guilford Press (pp. 406–21).

Schonert-Reichl, K. A., and Hymel, S. (2007). Educating the heart as well as the mind:
Social and emotional learning for school and life success. *Education Canada* 47:
20–25.

Seligman, M. E., and Csikzentmihalyi, M. (2000). Positive psychology: An introduction. *American Psychologist* 55: 5–14.

Seligman, M. E., Ernst, R. M., Gillham, C., Reivich, K., and Linkins, M. (2009). Positive education: Positive psychology and classroom interventions. *Oxford Review of Education* 35: 293–311

Sheldon, K. M., Boehm, J. K., and Lyubomirsky, S. (2012). Variety is the spice of happiness: the hedonic adaptation prevention (HAP) model. In I. Boniwell and S. David (Eds.), *Oxford handbook of happiness* (pp. 901–14). Oxford, England: Oxford University Press.

Smith, D. J., Schneider, B. H., Smith, P. K., and Ananiadou, K. (2004). The effectiveness of whole-school antibullying programmes: A synthesis of evaluation research. *School Psychology Review* 33: 548–561.

Spivak, A. L. and Farran, D. C. (2012). First-grade teachers behaviors and children's prosocial actions in classrooms. *Early Education and Development* 23: 623–39.

Wang, S., and Tamis-LeMonda, C. S. (2003). Do child-rearing values in Taiwan and the United States reflect cultural values of collectivism or individualism? *Journal of Cross-Cultural Psychology* 34: 629–42.

Weissberg, R. P., Durlak, J. A., Domitrovich, C. E., and Gulotta, T. P. (2015). Social and emotional learning: Past, present, and future. In R. Weissberg, C. Domitrovich, J. Durlak, and T. Gullotta (Eds.). *The Handbook of Social and Emotional Learning (SEL): Research and Practice.* New York: Guilford Press (pp. 3–19).

Williamson, A. A., Modecki, K. L., and Guerra, N. G. (2015). Social and emotional learning programs in high school. In R. Weissberg, C. Domitrovich, J. Durlak, and T. Gullotta (Eds.). *The Handbook of Social and Emotional Learning (SEL): Research and Practice.* New York: Guilford Press (pp. 181–96).

Zylowska, L., Smalley, S., and Schwartz, J. (2008). Mindfulness for Attention Deficit Hyperactivity Disorder. In F. Didonna (Ed.), *Clinical handbook of mindfulness.* New York: Springer.

Conclusion

Mindfulness, Critical Friendship, and the Art of Giving Way

Shawn Michael Bullock

As this volume draws to a close, I am compelled to bring my attention back to my first exposure to mindfulness training, which occurred when I was in early elementary school. I was happy to be enrolled in *judo* classes, a happiness that translated into a lifelong involvement with martial arts that continues to this day. My *sensei* (teacher) taught in a traditional Japanese way; we were taught to be respectful not only to her by listening to her instructions carefully, but also to the *dojo* by having our uniforms clean and our belts properly tied. A large picture of *judo* founder Jigaro Kano was in a place of reverence, mounted in the center of the front wall above the eye level of even the adult students. We were expected to be on the mats 10 minutes before class started so that we could loosen up and get blood flowing to our muscles. She watched us intently but she never interfered with the inevitable way that a group of small children will quickly begin to move chaotically in any open space.

When she shouted *kiotsuke*, however, we were required to immediately stop what we were doing and line up, according to rank, in a proper kneeling position with our hands placed on our thighs and our fingers pointing inward to that we were encouraged to sit up straight. *Sensei* adopted the same posture, facing us, and waited. When I first started my *judo* studies, I was convinced this was another way of adults making sure that we were not goofing around. I had been to both pre-school and kindergarten by this point and I knew the teacher trick of waiting for everyone to be quiet before giving instructions. Right away, though, I noticed that *sensei* waited for longer periods of time. It was agonizing at first; it did not take me long to notice that any fidgeting would simply make her prolong the time. After what seemed like an eternity, she would call out *"rei"* and we would bow to her. She bowed back to us, always starting slightly after we begun our bow. *Sensei* would then turn pivot quickly on her knees toward the picture of Jigaro Kano—a movement that was at once graceful and an indicator of her considerable martial expertise—and call out *"rei"* a second time. We all bowed to the founder of *judo*; that we did this in unison was significant to me even during my first class.

I did not, however, understand the purpose behind *kiotsuke* until just before I earned my second rank (*nikyu*) in *judo* many months later. In hindsight, it occurred to me that the conversation around *kiotsuke* may well have been a part of the rank examination. One day when it was my turn to stay after class for an extra ten minutes to sweep the mats—a tradition that helped to establish shared responsibility and a sense of respect for the *dojo*—and my *sensei* asked, "Why do we start class with *kiotsuke*?"

I stopped sweeping, startled by the question. I replied, "Because you want us to be quiet?"

"That is a part of it, yes, but there is a better reason."

I distinctly recall being overwhelmed with nervousness. As much as I liked being prepared in elementary school, I liked being prepared for *judo* even more. I did not want to look foolish. I am not sure how much time passed, but eventually *sensei* let me off the hook. Paraphrasing her words from over three decades ago:

> *Kiotsuke* might be translated as "attention" in English, but it is not the kind of attention you are used to seeing soldiers perform on television. *Kiotsuke* means you need to pay attention to your self. Pay attention to how you were feeling when you got here. Pay attention to the fact that whatever kind of day you have had and whatever you might expect for tomorrow, you need to shift your attention to *judo* now. Pay attention to the moment.

I remember thinking for a minute about her response before being asked to resume sweeping so that my father would not be kept waiting outside. At the time, I remember that *sensei's* comments meant that *kiotsuke* was about getting ready for *judo* class. Although I did not refer to this as a lesson in mindfulness until many years later, the idea of attention as a way or being present in the moment, and of being ready to learn, stuck with me almost right away. It was a touchstone that helped me get through many frustrating years of schooling, particularly in early elementary school.

As I grew up with and through martial arts, I learned more about what *kiotsuke* means and about other mindful practices embedded in these ancient traditions. The word itself breaks down in interesting ways if you consider its component parts, but a full discussion of its philosophical implication is outside the scope of the last chapter of this collection. For now, it is sufficient to consider that the word refers to a connectedness between all present in the room and between those who have come before us and those who will follow us. Each time *kiotsuke* was called in my *judo* classes, it was an invitation to be present and to consider the ways that our actions influence, and our influenced by others.

I would argue that although this kind of attention is central to any martial art, the arts descended from various forms of jujitsu, including judo, are somewhat unique in the sense that their very nomenclature encourages their practitioners to be mindful of those they interact with. Many people know that *judo* is literally translated as the *way of gentleness*. Fewer are aware that it could also be translated as the *art of giving way*. Fewer still are aware of Jigaro Kano's comments on the nature of this gentleness and giving way:

> Let us say that a man is standing before me whose strength is ten, and that my own strength is but seven. If he pushes me a hard as he can, I am sure to be pushed back or knocked down, even if I resist with all my might. This is opposing strength with strength. But if instead of opposing him I give way to the extent he has pushed, withdrawing my body and maintaining my balance, my opponent will lose his balance. Weakened by his awkward position, he will be unable to use all his strength. It will have fallen to three. Because I retain my balance, my strength remains at seven. Now I am stronger than my opponent and can defeat him by using only half my strength, keeping the other half available for some other purpose. *Even if you are stronger than your opponent, it is better to first give way.* By doing so you conserve energy while exhausting your opponent. (Kano, 1937/1994, pp. 16–17, emphasis added)

Kano is discussing what is popularly known as "using one's opponent's strength against them." A more accurate summary would be to state that that one must move in direction one is being pushed or pulled, at least initially. Balance is more important that strength

Some people might be uncomfortable with the combative elements of Kano's comments, or indeed to any use of martial arts as metaphors for thinking about academic work. In Bullock (2014), I demonstrated the value of considering informal learning experiences like these with respect to understanding my pedagogy of teacher education. Here I would add that martial arts are less about reacting to conflicts in the outside world than they are about responding to challenges in our inner lives. As Falkenberg points out in this volume, we are often quite unaware of our inner lives, even though they have ethical and moral dimensions to how we act in the world.

Many of the mindful practices embedded deeply in the Japanese martial arts I have studied, for example, are designed to help one through the kinds of challenges and barriers we throw up for ourselves. In my studies of *shotokan karate*, for example, I learned that the point of practicing the "basic" kicks and hand strikes over and over again, regardless of rank, was to realize that there was always something new to be learned even if one felt overwhelming familiarity with the technique. My *karate sensei* used to literally call out *mokuso* (meditate) the beginning and conclusion of every class, just after the bow. The word for meditate became an imperative verb.

Mindful action in dynamic circumstances can also be a form of meditation, even if it has applications that facilitate defending oneself. Kano (1937/1994) himself recognized that *judo* was about much more that self-defense or achieving proficiency in combat. He explicitly framed *judo* as physical education, which he defined as "making the body strong, useful, and healthy while building character through mental and moral discipline" (p. 20). Kano defined *judo* was about giving way, or gentleness, through efficient techniques. Kano felt that physical education needed to be similarly efficient in its use of "mental and physical energy," stating that "future advances in physical education will be made in conformity with this principle" (pp. 20–21). He also explicitly addressed the benefits of *judo* for ethical training, stating:

> *Judo* teaches us to look for the best possible course of action, whatever the individual circumstances, and helps us to understand that worry is a waste of energy. Paradoxically, the person who has failed and the person who is at the peak of success are in exactly the same position. Each must decide what to do next. (p. 23)

It is here that clear links to Schön's (1983) concept of reframing might be made. When an educator encounters a problem of practice, they must decide what to do next. A part of that decision will be based on tacit knowledge, but another part of the decision will be made in action, through process called reflection-in-action. There is also the opportunity to take action, and to see how the situation speaks back to the educator as a result of the action. So too is the process of open, unscripted training in judo, defined by Kano as *randori*.

My earliest lesson in mindfulness, then, led to both a lifelong passion for practicing and teaching martial arts and a powerful metaphor for thinking about learning and learning to teach. I needed to learn to come to attention (*kiotsuke*) about my self and my connection to other practitioners before I learned the art of giving way (*judo*). The common element to both of these concepts is that at least one partner is beneficial to more advanced practice. It is one thing, for example, to quiet one's mind alone at home, it is another to come to attention in a room full of people who are each bringing the experiences of their days with them into the *dojo*. I can practice falling correctly, *ukemi*, quite effectively on my own but it is quite another matter to learn to fall when being thrown by someone else. The matter is made even clearer when one engages in non-prescriptive open *randori* practice.

I have learned over the years that the art of giving way requires a training partner. Practicing with a partner makes us both responsible for the quality of our learning. If my partner interacts with me in a half-hearted way, I will develop unwarranted confidence in an improperly applied technique. Similarly, there are few things as exciting as training with someone who has expertise in an unfamiliar art, as my worldview is necessarily challenged and I am afforded the opportunity of coming to new conclusions. Training in martial arts requires the full commitment, the mindful attention, of both practitioners. Schnellert and Richardson (this volume) remind us of just how challenging, and important, it is for colleagues to engage in critical friendship to challenge each other's work by being present and attentive and thus, providing additional lenses with which to view professional development.

We might say that martial arts training requires us to act in ways that self-study practitioners expect of their critical friends. As Costa and Kallick (1993) noted, critical friendship means that both people are advocates for the success of the work—be it in *judo* training or in teacher education. Similarly, both *judo* practitioners and teacher educators are required to listen to each other and to respond to each other's learning needs with integrity. Perhaps most importantly, working with a critical friend in either system helps one to identify future learning needs. As Schuck and Russell (2005) stated:

> One problematic issue of self-study concerns the difficulty of assessing one's own practice and reframing it. Personal practice has grown out of the practitioner's belief system and thus tends to be comfortable. *It is often difficult to make changes or to ascertain if those changes have improved practice.* (p. 108, emphasis added)

A *judo* practitioner who has never worked with someone who challenges their movements or their approach to open practice will find it difficult to assess their learning. So too will the teacher educator who does not seek out the input of others for their own professional development.

The chapters presented in this volume explore several different varieties of critical friendship, offering many new insights that we hope are of use to those interested in the intersections between critical friendship, mindfulness, and professional development. The chapters have helped me begin to connect the dots between my own mindful practices as a martial artist and the role that critical friendship plays in my approach to self-study. For example, Makaiau, Wang, Ragoonaden, Leng, and De-Woody reminded me of the importance of challenging my assumptions about how texts that I often discuss with both teacher candidates and martial arts students are being interpreted, and the degree to which I am teaching in manners that are congruent with these texts and with my stated values. It was their chapter that prompted me to return to Jigaro Kano's book as a catalyst for constructing this chapter. Gilham outlines the connections between critical friendship, compassion, and equanimity—the last concept has particular resonance with the ideas of physical education espoused by Jigaro Kano. Binfet reminded me that kindness can come from mindful approaches. It would worthwhile for me to further explore connections between Kano's idea of giving way, gentleness, and kindness in my own work on the connections between martial arts and thinking about teaching and learning. The meta-critical friendship provided by O'Sullivan to Ní Chróinín and Fletcher has provided a catalyst for me to consider ways in which to invite other martial arts instructors into conversations with teacher educators, as there is something incredible valuable about a third person assisting in the development of a critical friendship—not least of which is O'Sullivan's positioning as a *connector of ideas.*

Perhaps part of the reason that I rely so heavily of critical friendship in my own work is that I learned about the value of others in mindful practice as a young martial artist. One of the things about self-study methodology that has always appealed to me is the idea that, although there is no one *right* way to do a self-study of practice (Loughran, 2005), there are a set of shared principles and beliefs. It makes sense that one might see a similar cluster of shared principles and beliefs around the idea of critical friendship and mindfulness. Rut Gísladóttir, Johnson Lachuck, and DeGraff (this volume) stated that some relatively straightforward principles, such as listening to others with respect are at the core of teacher education. As this reflection comes to a natural, but temporary conclusion, I am aware of how our inner and outer lives have permeated the multiple pathways of professional development. The chapters in this book posit that an innovative blend of critical friendship and mindfulness steeped in empathy, compassion, and kindness provide a supportive and nurturing framework upon which to reflect and to inform practice and praxis. Perhaps another foundational principle of a mindful approach to professional development might be the act of *kiotsuke*, coming together as critical friends and attending to the art of giving way, by sharing practiced wisdom and practical knowledge.

REFERENCES

Bullock, S. M. (2014). Exploring the impact of prior experiences in non-formal education on my pedagogy of teacher education. *Studying Teacher Education, 10*(2), 103–116.

Costa, A. L., and Kallick, B. (1993). Through the lens of a critical friend. *Educational Leadership, 51*(2), 49–51.

Kano, J. (1937/1994). *Kodokan judo.* Tokyo: Kodansha International.

Loughran, J. (2005). Researching teaching about teaching: Self-study of teacher education practices. *Studying Teacher Education, 1*(1), 5–16.

Schuck, S., and Russell, T. (2005). Self-study, critical friendship, and the complexities of teacher education. *Studying Teacher Education, 1*(2), 107–121.

Schön, D. A. (1983). *The reflective practitioner: How professionals think in action.* New York: Basic Books.

Index

IAK. *See Intentional Acts of Kindness*
ideas, 55–56, 85
identity, 2–3; in community, 67–68;
   pedagogy and, 16, 27–28
improvisational theatre, 18–19
Increased Educator Mental Health, 99
inner experiences: contemplative
   professional practice in, 7–8; Core
   Reflection Approach of, 6–7; of
   inner work, 6–7, 10; intelligent
   report of, 6–7
inner life, 2–4. *See also* teachers' inner
   life
inner wisdom, 9, 10n5
inner work: conceptualization of, 6;
   inner experiences of, 6–7, 10;
   mindfulness in, 8–9
inquiry, 18, 35; collaborative critical,
   22–23, 26; about eye contact, 69; in
   p4cHI, 62, 68–70, 72. *See also*
   personal inquiry stance
institutional constraints: ideas and,
   55–56; research and, 56; time in, 55
intelligent report, 6–7
Intentional Acts of Kindness (IAK):
   adaptation of, 113–114; mindfulness
   and, 111, 112, 113–114
interactivity, 78
interconnectivity, 22, 22–23
interrogator, 85–86
*Introduction to Academic Pedagogy: An
   Aboriginal Perspective* (EDUC 104),
   21–23
ishin-denshin (direct transmission), 9–10

Jackson, Thomas, 60
Jandér, K., 15, 64
Jardine, David, 97–98
Jasman, A. M., 17, 18, 19, 20, 26, 27, 28
Jaspers, Karl, 9
Johnson, R. A., 3
judgement. *See* practical judgement
judo, 122; critical friends in, 122–123,
   124; *kiotsuke* in, 119–120; meaning
   of, 121, 122

K–12, 107–108
Kabat-Zinn, J., 72
Kallick, B., 15, 18, 19–20, 72, 123

Kano, Jigaro, 119–120, 121, 122, 123; on
   ethics, 122; on giving way, 121
Kanpol, B., 16
Kearney, R., 27–28
kindness: academics with, 112; benefits
   of, 113–114; bullying and, 112–113;
   mindfulness related to, 110–114;
   research on, 111–112
kiotsuke (attention to self), 119–120, 124
Kitchen, J., 26
knowledge generation, 28
Korthagen, F. A. J., 6
Kretchmar, R. Scott, 77

LaBoskey, Vicki Kubler, 78
labour force, 110
Lacasse, R., 26
Lakoff, G., 3
Lane, P., 22
Lasalle, H. M. E., 9
*Learning About Meaningful Physical
   Education* (LAMPE): authenticity in,
   82–83; meta-critical friend in, 79, 83;
   metaphors and, 79–80, 85;
   mindfulness and, 78, 80, 81; PETE
   and, 77, 79, 84, 87; S-STEP in, 77,
   81–82, 84, 87; tension in, 78, 80–81,
   81–82; vulnerability in, 78, 81–82
letting go, 101
life, 2–4; as metaphor, 79–80, 81, 83, 87.
   See also teachers' inner life
linguistic diversity, 52–54
Lipman, Matthew, 60
Loughran, J., 28, 29, 47
Lytle, S., 14, 27–28

Macintyre Latta, M., 17–18, 47, 73
Malhotra-Bentz, V., 35
marginalization, 23
McCown, D., 94
McMindfulness: corporations and,
   95–96; dysregulation and, 96–98; in
   MIE, 95–98; secularity of, 95–96;
   self-regulation and, 96
mediator, 86–87
meditate (*mokuso*), 121
meditation, 8–9. *See also* mindfulness
Mental Health Education, 92

self-correction, 71
self-regulation, 96
self-study, 73, 78; metaphors in, 16–18.
    See also specific topics
Self-Study of Teacher Education
    Practices (S-STEP): critical friends
    in, 64; in LAMPE, 77, 81–82, 84, 87;
    MT in, 64–65; p4cHI and, 63–65
Selwyn, N., 25
Senge, 93
sensei (teacher), 119–120
Shapiro, J., 35
shotokan karate, 121
shushing response, 4, 5, 7–8
simplicity, 56
skepticism, 25
skills, 107, 110
Smith, D. J., 113
Snowden, Edward, 24
social and emotional learning (SEL),
    108; benefits of, 109–110; CASEL
    and, 109; definition of, 109; for
    employees, 110; five pillars of, 109;
    K–12 and, 107–108; mindfulness in,
    110–114; soft skills in, 107, 110;
    stress and, 108; teachers and, 108.
    See also kindness
social competencies, 26
social justice, 41–42
soft skills, 107, 110
spaces, 35, 101
special needs students, 27, 54
S-STEP. *See* Self-Study of Teacher
    Education Practices
STEP. *See* Secondary Teacher
    Education Program
stress, 108; equanimity in, 101; letting
    go of, 101; power and, 101; reactions
    to, 101; space in, 101; in themes,
    100–101. *See also* tension
subconscious, 3
Swaffield, S., 15, 73

Tang, C. S., 73
Teacher Education Programs, 13
teachers (*sensei*), 108, 119–120; in axial
    age, 9–10; in Canada, 10; as
    employees, 9; MT for, 64–65. *See also*
    specific topics

teachers' inner life, 1–2; automatic
    routines and, 4–5; ethics and, 5–6
teacher's strike, 69
Teaching Mindfulness (McCown, Reibel,
    and Micozzi), 94
team, 35–36
techne (technical knowledge), 13–14, 17
telling moments: control in, 40;
    exclusion in, 40; in mindful
    relational professional
    development, 38–40; tension in, 38,
    39, 40
tension, 46; in cultural diversity, 53–55;
    in LAMPE, 78, 80–81, 81–82; in
    mindful relational professional
    development, 36, 38, 39, 42; in
    telling moments, 38, 39, 40
themes, 99, 102; critical friends in, 100;
    openness as, 101; stress in, 100–101
theory, 47–48, 61
therapy dogs, 108
Thornburg, D. D., 79, 87
thoughts, 3
Tibetan Buddhism, 97–98
time, 68–69; in readers theater script,
    49–50, 51, 55, 56
travel agent/tour guide, 17, 18; holistic
    pedagogy and, 23; pedagogy and,
    27
Trungpa, Chogyam, 97, 97–98
trust, 100

unawareness, 3
unscripted training (*randori*), 122

Van der Rijst, R. M., 16–17
Van Driel, J. H., 16–17
Varela, F. J., 2–3
Verloop, N., 16–17
Visser, A., 16–17
Visser-Wijnveen, G. J., 16–17
vulnerability, 101; in LAMPE, 78, 81–82

waterhole, 79, 79–80, 81, 83
Weissberg, R. P., 109
wisdom, 9, 10n5, 13–14, 17
world, 68

Yennie-Donmoyer, J., 49

About the Editor and Contributors

Karen Ragoonaden is a member of the Faculty of Education of the University of British Columbia's Okanagan Campus, Canada. She has lived, studied, and worked in North America, Europe, and Africa. Her publications and research interests lie in the area of the Scholarship of Teaching and Learning with a focus on French Education, Aboriginal Education, Critical Pedagogy, and Self-Study of Teacher and Teacher Education practices (S-STEP). As a qualified Yoga instructor, the concept of Mindfulness in Education is an integral component of her research and her practice. As a university educator and researcher, her focus and commitment to educational leadership and curricular innovation have been recognized by virtue of her on campus, professional, and community work relating to equity, diversity, and inclusion.

Shawn Michael Bullock is an assistant professor of science education at Simon Fraser University in British Columbia, Canada and a professional physicist. He uses self-study methodology to explore the relationships between self and self-in-practice in much of his work. Shawn is currently investigating the ways in which his lifelong practice as a martial artist has influenced his approach to teaching future teachers.

Thomas Falkenberg is an associate professor in the Faculty of Education at the University of Manitoba, Canada. He is the current the Coordinator of the Education for Sustainable Well-Being Research Group at the University of Manitoba (www.eswbrg.org). His current research focuses on the notion of teaching as contemplative professional practice and on understanding and assessing well-being and well-becoming in schools. More details about his research and academic background can be gleaned from http://home.cc.umanitoba.ca/~falkenbe/index.html.

Pamela Richardson is a practitioner-scholar passionate about connecting inner transformation with social change through education. She is curious about how holistic personal-professional development grounded in arts-based, mindful and living inquiry practices might enliven and deepen academic life and community. She has published in the areas of poetic and arts-based inquiry; self-study and professional development; and, giftedness and talent development. Pamela is an assistant professor in the School of Education and Technology at Royal Roads University, where she is head of the Master's in Educational Leadership and Management program

Leyton Schnellert researches teacher learning, practice, and collaboration. In particular he examines how teachers and teaching and learners and learning can mindfully attend to student diversity, self and co-regulated learning, and place-consciousness. Dr. Schnellert is the Pedagogy and Participation research cluster lead in the University of British Columbia's Okanagan campus Institute for Community Engaged Research and Co-Chair of British Columbia's Rural Education Advisory.

Karen Rut Gísladóttir is an assistant professor in the School of Education at the University of Iceland. Her research interest lies in the area of sociocultural theories of literacy teaching and learning. Karen has ten years of experience teaching in the Icelandic school system, as teacher of children who are deaf and as a teacher educator. Karen has engaged in self-study to improve her practice both as an elementary teacher and as a teacher educator.

Amy Johnson Lachuk is an associate professor of literacy education at Hunter College, City University of New York, USA. Amy completed her doctoral degree at the University of Wisconsin-Madison in literacy studies. Amy has eighteen years of experience in teaching and working with educators in urban and rural schools. Amy is the author of a *Field Guide for Beginning Literacy Teachers,* a workbook intended to connect theory and practice while beginning teachers are completing fieldwork experiences.

Tricia DeGraff is the principal at Academy for Integrated Arts, an arts integrated, constructivist, inquiry-based elementary school. Tricia completed her doctoral degree at the University of Missouri–Kansas City (UMKC), USA and teaches in the teacher education program at UMKC as an adjunct professor. Tricia has eighteen years of experience in urban schools as a classroom teacher, teacher educator, and school leader.

Amber Strong Makaiau is the Director of Curriculum and Research at the University of Hawai'i Uehiro Academy for Philosophy and Ethics in Education. She is a dedicated philosophy for children Hawai'i practitioner who achieved National Board Certification while teaching secondary social studies in the Hawaii State Department of Education for over ten years. Her current projects include designing and researching a brand new Philosophic Inquiry course, experiments with deliberative pedagogy, a philosophy for children Hawai'i international self-study research collective, and working with pre-service social studies teachers in the UH College of Education.

Jessica Ching-Sze Wang is an associate professor in the Department of Education at National Chiayi University, Taiwan. She is specialized in John Dewey's philosophy of education and is the author of *John Dewey in China: To Teach and to Learn* (SUNY, 2007). She has been practicing p4cH in Taiwan at the elementary and college level since 2013 and has won her university's Teaching Excellence Award in 2015 for integrating p4cH to undergraduate teaching. Her current research interests include constructing the educational theory of p4cH in light of Dewey, reviving Confucian philosophy through P4C, and exploring the aesthetic and moral dimensions of the p4cH approach to education.

Lu Leng is an assistant professor at the University of Guangzhou, China. Graduating from the Educational Psychology Department at the University of Hawai'i at Manoa, she engaged in philosophy for children Hawai'i (p4cHI) practice, research and trainings in China. Her research interests include comparative research on p4cHI, survey questionnaire design and validation, educational program evaluation, and psychological development in childhood and adolescence. Her current project is to develop a questionnaire on children's psychological and emotional development and provide p4cHI trainings for the HappyBox educational institution in Beijing.

Heather M. DeWoody earned her master's degree in educational psychology and is faculty at the University of Hawai'i, College of Education specializing in educational research. She is researching *mindfulness in education* and *meta-mindfulness* for her dissertation, specifically examining philosophy for children Hawaii's (p4cHI) educational model. Heather is a long-time practitioner of meditation and yoga and is actively involved in Hawaii's community working with several non-profits that facilitate mindful practices and collaborations.

Déirdre Ní Chróinín is a physical education teacher educator at the elementary level and Head of the Department of Arts Education and Physical Education, Mary Immaculate College, University of Limerick, Ireland. Déirdre's research explores young people's experiences in physical education and sport settings as well as the preparation of their teachers and coaches. She coordinates the Teacher Educator Self-Study Initiative at Mary Immaculate College and is co-chair of the Active Schools/Active Communities Research Cluster of the PEPAYS Ireland Research Centre.

Mary O'Sullivan is the Professor of Physical Education and Youth Sport at the University of Limerick (UL), Ireland and co-founder of the PEPAYS-Ireland Research Centre. She is the former Dean of Education and Health Sciences at UL and a former Associate Dean of the College of

Education at The Ohio State University. Mary's research interests are in teacher learning with a particular interest in school university partnerships in teacher education, teacher educators and professional development for teachers.

Tim Fletcher is Assistant Professor in the Department of Kinesiology at Brock University, Canada. Tim is an active member of the self-study research community regularly contributing to Studying Teacher Education, the Castle Conference, and the S-STEP Special Interest Groups at the American Educational Research Association and Canadian Society for Studies in Education annual conferences. He is on the International Advisory Board for *Studying Teacher Education: A journal of self-study of teacher education practices* and sits on the Editorial Board for Physical Education and Sport Pedagogy. Tim's research interests are in teacher/teacher educator socialization and identity, pre-service teacher education, and self-study of practice.

Chris Gilham is Assistant Professor in the Faculty of Education at St. Francis Xavier University, Antigonish, Nova Scotia, Canada. He is a former junior high/elementary school teacher and consultant. His work is focused on helping cultivate spaces in school settings where typically marginalized and codified students and their educators can thrive together.

John-Tyler Binfet is an assistant professor in the Faculty of Education at the University of British Columbia, Okanagan. His research examines conceptualizations of school kindness and his work on kindness has been published in *Psychology in the Schools*, the *International Journal of Emotional Education*, and *Canadian Children*. Dr. Binfet is the lead author of the *School Kindness Scale*, a 5-item measure assessing students' perceptions of school kindness. Additionally, Dr. Binfet is the director of the *Building Academic Retention through K9s* (B.A.R.K., www.barkubc.ca) program and oversees 45 therapy dogs on campus who provide social and emotional support to undergraduate students facing challenges around stress and homesickness.